Praise *for* *The Table of Life*

"Tommi Vincent is one of the most inspiring women I know—a fierce mother, a gifted cook, and a generous soul. *The Table of Life* is her love letter to resilience, community, and finding purpose, and it's exactly the nourishment we all need right now."

—*Kerry Diamond*, founder of Cherry Bombe and host of *Radio Cherry Bombe*

"Tommi is the epitome of class, strength, and wisdom. I am beyond thrilled to see Tommi package her wisdom in the format of a book. I recommend *The Table of Life* to any woman desiring to lead a life pleasing to God and to build a family home culture on Christian principles."

—*Teneshia Warner*, CEO of EGAMI Group

"Chef Tommi, armed with a pot of healing food and wisdom, serves her gifted talents to those she shelters with love, kindness, and abundant grace. An oasis in an apron, feeding the souls and spirits of so many who are fortunate to gather at her table, she conjures up the power and beauty of food in every serving . . . and her healing joy excites us with every bite we take. Chef, keep doing what you're doing with dignity and grace, and save a plate of your goodness for me!"

—*Alexander Smalls*, James Beard Award–winning chef, cookbook author, and raconteur

amplify

www.amplifypublishinggroup.com

The Table of Life: Nourishing the Soul with Food, Love, and Faith

Some names and identifying details have been changed to protect the privacy of individuals. All recipes have been tested and used successfully by the author, but results may vary. The author and publisher advise readers to take full responsibility for their nutrition and diet and know their restrictions. Before cooking the recipes described in this book, be sure to evaluate the ingredients for any possible allergies or interactions, and do not bake beyond your level of skill or comfort level. Readers should always follow best practices for safe food preparation. The publisher and the author assume no responsibility for errors, inaccuracies, omissions, or any other inconsistencies herein. All such instances are unintentional and the author's own.

Tablescape Designer: Priscila Hawn
Photographer: Dominique Montreal Cooper

For more information, please contact:
Amplify Publishing, an imprint of Amplify Publishing Group
620 Herndon Parkway, Suite 220
Herndon, VA 20170
info@amplifypublishing.com

Library of Congress Control Number: 2025900251

CPSIA Code: PRV0625A

ISBN-13: 978-1-63755-930-7

Printed in the United States

This book is dedicated to my younger self. Thank you for surviving. Your courage, resilience, and strength made it possible for me to thrive today. I will continue to make you proud.

TOMMI A. VINCENT

The TABLE OF LIFE

Nourishing the Soul with Food, Love, and Faith

amplify

CONTENTS

Foreword

To be fed from the kitchen of Tommi Vincent is a holy welcome. It is the invitation that one receives when entering a house of worship. And worship often happens outside of the religious temples we've grown accustomed to. A faith-based space can come in many forms: sister circles, kitchen tables, living room study sessions, online prayer gatherings, mutual aid collective platforms, and within your chosen family's arms. I learned this firsthand as a guest of Tommi's, during her annual women's retreat. During the hot summer wellness retreat, I sat at the table surrounded by the warmth of women's laughter. Within the folds of their sisterly knowing, we broke bread, shared vulnerable moments of our own becoming, and prayed for one another with a fervor so real, the walls must've shaken! Or maybe it was just the table we all shared that shook from the weight of goodness placed on its bones. These miraculous meals were various pots of seafood steaming of butter, or personal-sized sweet potato soufflé, or blue southern steeped-in-heaven grits—they sated us. Our souls were comforted. Our stomachs filled with songs and glorious testaments of survival. Our cups clinked in celebration as we let this feeling of faith in our sisters' glow be a reflection of God's love. This moment of seeing was prepared by the heart and hands of Tommi.

Have you had someone pray for you? It is an honor and as generous as lamb's wool. A prayer from one human to another, in request of your hardships being lifted, or your heart feeling the weight of worth and light is an absolute gift. And as freeing as it feels to be prayed for and to send active prayers, it is not common. Enter Tommi A. Vincent. I met Tommi through community building, and after one poem and one meal, we became chosen folks.

> And he has given us this command: Anyone who loves God must also love their brother and sister.
>
> – John 4:21

Tommi taught me that what it means to love God is to love your sisters. Tommi taught me through food and gathering the root principles of His love. Through food and fellowship, Tommi taught me to tap into the source to reveal my true capacity for love.

Mahogany L. Browne, BKLYN 2025
Author/Poet-in-Residence, Lincoln Center

Introduction

Take a Seat, Stay a While

We all have a story to tell. One that lives within us, whether we know it or not.

Come sit, stay a while, so that I may share mine.

I learned how to cook, love, and pray in Eggert's Crossing Village in Lawrenceville, New Jersey. It was a little town just outside of Trenton and not far from Philadelphia. I absolutely loved living there.

Learning How to Cook

As the youngest of four siblings, there were many hands responsible for taking care of me. On one dreary, rainy day when I was three years old, my siblings and I all lay on the cold tiles of our living room floor, snuggled in blankets and watching Saturday morning cartoons. What a time to be a kid!

"Make me some hot cereal!" I exclaimed.

No one moved.

I moseyed my little toddler self into the kitchen, pulled up a chair, and proceeded to prepare what seemed like the staple meal of our home, Farina. Like Cream of Wheat but a bit finer in texture and no brown specks, Farina was and still is my favorite hot cereal. I remember this moment like it was yesterday.

We had a white aluminum dinette set with orangish-red laminated seats. I dragged a chair from the dinette table and pulled my little self onto it to get the hot cereal out of the cabinet. The pots sat on the stovetop. I just needed to select the one I thought best. I watched my oldest sister make Farina all the time, so I knew to choose the smallest saucepan with a wiggly handle.

I leaned my body over the counter as far as I could stretch to reach the faucet to add water into the pot. I placed the pot on the burner, mimicking all the steps I saw my big sister do: I tipped the box over to pour the cereal into the pot.

Not having a concept of how much or how quickly to pour, nor the dexterity to pour and stir at the same time, my hot cereal was full of uncooked lumps of Farina. One part I did not take note of when my big sister cooked Farina was that the water should be boiling.

Cold, raw lumps, but I was proud and enjoyed every spoonful. This was the very first meal I ever cooked.

Learning How to Love

Christmas that year was memorable for two reasons.

The first is that I got the red boom box with a yellow microphone I had asked for from Santa. The second is that I witnessed domestic violence for the first time.

As I sat on the tiled floor of my bedroom playing with my boom box, the door flung open. My eyes widened, full of curiosity and fear. I watched as a beloved family member—bloodied, naked, trembling, and out of breath—jumped behind the door for safety. No words, no sounds, just me looking at her and her not looking at me.

As a matter of fact, no one spoke of this moment ever again. The police took the perpetrator away, only for him to return later that evening. He remained part of her life, and I was left to make sense of this story in my young mind.

My takeaway: This was love. Love showed up as hurt and pain. Although this moment solidified my first definition of love, many additional moments ingrained in our family culture would shape how I understood and redefined love as I grew older.

Learning How to Pray

One summer day when I was three years old, my mom announced that she was taking us to the beach.

Woohoo! I thought.

She sent my three siblings and me to get ready. Everything was going smoothly until I could not find my shoe. I ran down-stairs to let my mom know.

She shouted loudly enough for everyone to hear, "We are not leaving this house until Tommi finds her shoe."

My eyes welled up with tears, and I searched my room high and low. No shoe! I slid myself down the closet wall until I was sitting on the floor, crisscross applesauce. With tears streaming down my face, I cried out, "God, help me find my shoe!"

That is my first memory of knowing that I believed in someone greater than anyone on all the earth. I don't remember if I ever found my shoe. That wasn't the point. What I do remember is that was my first prayer. I was someone who believed.

A Trinity of Ingredients

Although my introductions to these three concepts were rough around the edges, food, love, and prayer have become my recipe for living a seasoned life. Not the love I learned at three years old but the love I grew to know—real love that does not hurt intentionally. Subsequently, I've found myself gravitating toward fellowship at the table. I can show my love for others through cooking soul-comforting meals like the women in my family have done for generations. The table is where I take a pulse check to understand how everyone is doing and to identify whether someone needs resuscitation. A delicious meal with loved ones eases life's challenges and makes way for vulnerability. Understanding how life is affecting others helps me to know how to pray. Prayer is a vital tool for me. You can find me in my prayer room just off my kitchen bright and early every morning.

Although cooking, love, and prayer are my tools, my hope is that this book will inspire and encourage you to identify the tools that will assist you in living a seasoned life. In this book, I'll share stories from my life as well as ideas to help you build your table with tasty recipes that nourish the soul.

I cooked that first meal by myself at the age of three, but most of my cooking lessons came from the women in my family as I grew older. Learning how to cook at the feet of these seasoned women in my family was a lifesaver. Cooking became my primary self-soothing tactic during major pivotal points in my life, including when I delivered my first daughter at the age of twelve, when I escaped an abusive relationship in my late teens, and many years later when I recognized that I needed the assistance of a mental health professional to help with my depression.

As I reflect on the many occasions when my mom, nanas,

and aunts created warm, comforting spaces filled with belly-deep laughter, delicious food, and heartfelt memories in the midst of addictions, abuse, and poverty, I'm flooded with unmeasured appreciation. It's no small feat to continue to love through pain and sadness. It's no wonder I was able to rise above my depression. I come from good stock! The women in my family are strong, stoic, and secure. They influenced me tremendously. They instilled valuable insights into me as a child, and I'm grateful for the nourishing environments they created for our family that fed both our souls and our stomachs. Our family gatherings were anchored by tasty food laid out on the table, accompanied by meaningful conversations.

I honor them to this day every time I grace a table inspired by my mother, Pamela, Nana Edie, Nana Claudia, Mom (great-grandmother), Aunt Cissy, Aunt Alverna, Aunt Dolline, Aunt Lucy, Aunt Lucille, Aunt Nanny, Mrs. Vincent, and all the other women who added seasoning to my life. It's a constant reminder that the best recipes have a little bit of this, a pinch of that, and, most importantly, a whole lot of love.

Legacies and Heirlooms

In this book, we'll start with the foundation of a legacy.

I was overjoyed and quite smitten when I met my husband, Troy, and we were able to start building our legacy together, one that included food, cooking, and shared recipes. Cooking and eating are the through lines in our lives. Even in difficult times, when life has rocked my world, I've been encouraged to pass along legacy-inspired recipes to my family and future generations to experience. We are afforded the opportunity to carry forward the lessons of our ancestors.

I believe that recipes are heirlooms. My family did not share written recipes. They cooked from the soul. I learned by watching, then by experiencing the feeling of a warm hug that the food invoked. These treasured memories inspired my recipes. I'm blessed to be able to introduce my family to relatives they may not have met in person by cooking the dishes those relatives added to our family tradition. We experience their love in every dish I prepare. My ancestors' legacy continues through my recipes.

Troy and I married in 1994 when I was nineteen and he was twenty-three. It all happened so fast! Troy was thoughtful, kind, and handsome. I found him irresistible. I'd never experienced love in this way before. Admittedly, I was bracing myself for the boogeyman to show up. He never came. Troy made me feel loved, special, and valued. We fell madly in love after meeting in college and launched into the deep together, despite the naysayers who were convinced that I was not the right woman to be his wife.

Troy was a professional athlete in the National Football League, which meant there was some terrain that a young girl from Trenton, New Jersey, had zero experience navigating. But I trusted myself to learn fast so that I could support him. It was straight on-the-job training, and I was determined to excel. It was difficult to gain the acceptance and approval of people who were determined to be against me, but I still tried to win them over with Troy by my side. For the longest time, I wondered how people could dislike me when they didn't know me. But I tried not to speculate on the reasoning. In the brief moments when I allowed my mind to go there, I chalked it up to one of two reasons:

They didn't like that I was a teenage mother.

They thought they were protecting Troy from someone they didn't consider worthy.

Thankfully, Troy never listened to anyone else's opinions. He stuck by me just as I stuck by him.

"It's you and me, babe," he would say then and still says today.

Making Mindful Choices

As Troy and I built our life together, we moved quite a few times. It was the nature of his line of work. I took great pride in creating a home base for my family and in maintaining stability no matter where we landed. This allowed our children to settle into their school communities and develop friendships.

My decision was met with opposition from family and friends who chastised me for being a stay-at-home mother. It didn't matter to them that when I was growing up, both of my parents worked, which was hard on my siblings and me. I remember being in elementary school and having friends whose moms had the opportunity to stay at home, and I aspired to do the same. My Nana Claudia was also a stay-at-home mom, and my memories of her life made me want to follow in her footsteps. When I wasn't feeling well, my mom would drop me at her home on her way to work. I would watch Nana Claudia see my aunt off on the school bus, then care for the home, prepare lunch, and cap it off with an episode of *The Young and The Restless*. I remember thinking, *I want to do this!*

Those memories were still strong when I was a young mom and wife. So when I heard people's objections to my life choices, I was able to stand my ground. I do my best to operate from a platform that centers me and that allows my gifts to show up. I work to discipline myself to avoid focusing on the external; intentionally giving focus to the internal is a daily effort. My thoughts and decisions are based on the belief that if I was sent somewhere,

I was meant to be there. That includes being a happy, fulfilled stay-at-home mother and wife.

Of course, that didn't mean every moment was easy. I experienced frustration, despair, and burnout, just like everyone. And the older I got, the more I saw that life was often hard and demanding for the women in my life. I learned from the best of them to keep your head up and to "make it do what it do." Often when I meet women, I wonder how many feet of water they're treading. You might think that if you can tread water, you'll be just fine, but you can't tread water forever. You'll become exhausted. Rest will become necessary; otherwise, you'll start sinking.

I didn't receive this lesson from someone else. I learned through experience. As a mature woman, I now see that the resiliency of the women in my family was what helped them tread deep water. I'm grateful that I inherited their strength. As a matter of fact, I'm very proud to have them etched into my DNA. I'm adding to the curriculum. I'm determined to share this lesson with my daughters and with every woman willing to listen. There is no honor in being a self-aggrandized martyr. We can choose to swim to the peaceful shore.

This book is about those lessons. It's about showing how I refused to sink and how I fought back—and how I believe you can too. There was a time in my life when I was holding on to nothing and had given up hope. When I entered into a personal relationship with God and started learning of him, with the guide of the Bible, it became the foundation of my principles. Your belief system drives your actions; everything you believe will inspire you to work to make your vision come true. Whatever you believe shapes the life you create for yourself. I've lived this truth and want to show you how to do the same.

So come sit as I share how I built and maintained my table, then filled it full of the nourishment required for me to move beyond surviving to thriving. Be inspired to build your own table for yourself that nourishes. Every chapter offers a new dish, full of a pinch of this and a pinch of that.

In these pages, I'll reflect on three pivotal moments of my life: becoming a mother at the age of twelve, dangling off a bridge at the hands of my abusive boyfriend, and experiencing a dark depression that turned the light off in my mind. In each of these moments, I thought to myself, *I'm not going to make it.* But I always did. My story is not one of tragedy but of triumph. All the ingredients of my life came together one dish at a time, setting a bountiful table full of wisdom and life experience that I'm eager to share here. It's filled with the words I wish I'd had the benefit of knowing as I embarked on womanhood.

We all have moments in life that pave the road of our journey. Had I stopped and surrendered to the tough moments I encountered along the way, I wouldn't be the woman I am today. I wouldn't be where I am now. There is a tremendous opportunity to learn, grow, and become in the hard places. My sincere hope is that when you read the final word of this book, like me, you'll believe that life is happening *for* you and not *to* you. Sometimes we win, sometimes we lose, but always we learn.

Come along with me as we learn to create a seasoned life filled with food, love, and faith.

Chapter One

Life Is Hard

> I can be changed by what happens to me.
> But I refuse to be reduced by it.
>
> —*Maya Angelou, Letter to My Daughter*

How did I get here?

It's a Monday morning, and I lie nestled in my blankets, cocooned in my sorrow. I need to get up. My eight-year-old twins must get to school. Troy is in New York for work, as he is most weekdays. The thought of being pulled into the principal's office to be reprimanded again for the twins arriving late makes me want to burrow deeper into my pillow-top mattress. Even though it's no longer fluffy. The pillow top has been reshaped with a permanent indentation of my body from the countless hours I've spent trying to escape from God knows what.

What is wrong with me?

The river of tears has dried up and left me like a fish out of water, gasping for air to fill my soul with life. I'm barely breathing and feel lifeless. I must get up. Walking down the hall to wake the twins less than twenty-five feet away feels like a marathon.

"It's time to turn it on, Tommi," I command myself.

"Good morning, good morning. Wake up, Mommy's babies!" I sing. How dare I even think about depriving them of joy? It doesn't matter how I feel. Their happiness is my priority.

I move to the laundry room to maintain my routine of one load of laundry per day, to prevent the dirty clothes from piling up. Turning on my gospel music to the highest volume but unable to mumble a single lyric, my body falls limp against the washing machine.

I'm not going to make it, I think as the tears dry on my face. *God, I need a lifeline!*

Have you ever been exercising, and you find it hard to breathe? Your heart is pounding out of your chest, and a bit of panic sets in. You desperately want to catch your breath. Instinctually, you stop, place your hands on your hips, bend over at the waist, and frantically breathe in and out. Desperation for breath while still breathing causes even more panic to set in. Your breathing has lost the rhythm of life.

That's how I felt, slumped against the washer. Like something as simple as breathing had become impossible. I thought to myself again, *I'm not going to make it.*

What was happening to me? Why couldn't I get it together? How could I not know what was going on in my own life? Moreover, how could I not know how to fix it? I remember feeling hugely disappointed in myself. For someone who wore strength as a banner, this sudden inability to cope was devastating.

Insight from Outside

I did not fully understand the gravity of that moment until recently, as I sat in on a book talk by Sheila Johnson for her memoir, *Walk through Fire*. Sheila read an excerpt about her mom setting her life aside for the sake of her family and later experiencing a mental breakdown. Sheila vowed to herself that she would never repeat what she had witnessed growing up, only to find herself in a similar position to her mom's.

There was something about hearing Sheila recount her story that opened my heart and allowed me to see this moment in my life more clearly than ever. I looked back on that scene in the laundry room and realized it was a turning point. My life was never the same after that.

I was in a very dark place. My ability to numb my feelings so that I could press through the hard things in my life had taken a toll. The truth is that the twins were late for school every single day. I convinced the principal that my challenges with fibroids—heavy bleeding for fifteen days out of the month—had me feeling fatigued and lifeless. All true statements. But I felt tired and unresponsive all the time, with no zeal to get out of bed on the good days of the month either.

As Sheila read from her book, it felt like she was reading about me. My womb was dying, my spirit was dying, and it was too much for me to bear. My eyes opened to see that during that time in my life, I was literally falling apart, and I was still giving everything I had to ensure that everyone around me was good. I was concerned about the principal, worried about how this was affecting my children, making sure the laundry was done, and whatever else was required of me to take care of everyone but myself. I had become a self-appointed, aggrandized martyr. I was prepared to die on this hill. Just like Sheila's mom and Sheila herself, I had set my life aside for the sake of my family and had driven myself to a mental breakdown.

Benefiting from the wisdom of women like Sheila is always a timely blessing. I've been extremely fortunate to walk with amazing women throughout my adulthood. But as amazing as we were, we lacked the fundamental understanding that life is hard. We'd never cut ourselves any slack, stopped to rest, or asked for help. We became so accustomed to managing all that life threw our way that we made "hard" our friend, and we missed opportunities to course-correct before it was too late.

Each year, I host the Vincent Country Women's Retreat at my family's cabin in North Carolina. A few years ago at one of these events, three of the twenty seats were solid wood while the others were soft upholstered seating. I looked at my chair and thought, *It's hard.* This gave my brain the opportunity to process that knowledge. I sat for hours understanding this truth and didn't have to revisit the discussion with myself again. I was mentally prepared because I had acknowledged beforehand that the chair was hard. Meanwhile, the women seated on my left and my right wiggled and squirmed. The more they complained, the greater their discomfort mounted.

Two thoughts came to mind:

I knew at that very moment that this was a lesson worth sharing.

Why didn't anyone ever teach me this lesson?

Acknowledging that life is hard helps you prepare and adjust for the journey ahead. It sets your expectations in a reasonable way, which allows you to change your behavior. But back in the laundry room, I didn't know that. I glazed over this truth and worked to manage the hard instead of making changes to mitigate the difficult things in my life. I found myself in a mental crisis, unable to process a way out without the intervention of professional help.

How many times do we succumb to defeat before we acknowledge the truth of our situation? I'm not minimizing how difficult it is to be honest with ourselves. It took the lights going out in my soul before I could see myself. I could see the needs of my husband and children clearly. In one of the darkest moments of my life, I could see the need to provide clean socks and underwear for the twins, but I couldn't see my way out from under the covers I pulled over my head for the majority of the day. Honesty requires looking at ourselves, facing the person in the mirror. I shudder thinking about that! This isn't easy, especially if you don't have high regard for yourself. We conquer ourselves in our minds before life even has a chance to grind us down.

Many Faces of Depression

My depression was not the result of one thing. It was the result of many things that happened throughout the course of my life. Not getting out of bed was one of my symptoms, not the cause. Now when I find myself not wanting to get out of bed, I take a self-inventory. I have better tools to cope with that particular symptom. Others are still hard to manage.

For example, I was recently triggered by a situation that brought up memories from my past and caused me a great deal of heartache and pain. Most of the time, I think I'm good. But as soon as this incident reenters my thoughts or I see the person responsible, I find myself right back in the moment, as if it had just happened. Packing up my bags full of the issues of my life,

I move into the corner room of my mind. The situation repeats like a broken record. My mind goes into motion like a runaway train, speeding toward a head-on collision. All I can do is wait it out and let my thoughts calm down. It may be my mind that's making all this happen, but I still feel helpless to stop it.

I felt equally helpless to stop the broken record of overwhelm and exhaustion that was playing in my head back in the laundry room. But I also knew that it had to end for my personal well-being. Something needed to change because what I was doing was just making things worse.

For many years I operated through counterfeit strength. I trained myself to say the right things, fix my face, and bury my heartache and pain. I was a professional actor giving Oscar-worthy performances. As a woman of faith, it was easy to use my religion as a disguise. I was familiar with all the correct language that made me a Christian.

"All is well with my soul."

"All things work together for the good of those who love God."

"God fights my battles."

Although I believe in those statements, the truth was that I did not believe them for my personal struggle. God would make it work for everyone but me. I was damaged goods. I was unworthy. I was responsible for the choices that led to my depression, and I would reap the consequences.

My system was malfunctioning. Despite my valiant effort to continue my morning routine with the twins, depression got the best of me. I had developed this can-do attitude when the truth was that I could not. I could not take it anymore. I could not pretend anymore. I could not act like everything was OK anymore. I'd learned how to show up in most hard situations—at home, at church, at work, in public—by calling up my counterfeit strength. My depression wore a very convincing mask. No one knew the magnitude and depth of my struggle because I had the act mastered.

There were consequences for those around me as well. I felt resentment toward them. I believed they were responsible for not seeing how I struggled to survive. I expected them to be mind readers and to use X-ray vision to see into my broken heart. Every weekend our family plopped down on the sofa to watch television and talk about the week. Although everyone else giggled when telling their stories, I was as quiet as a church mouse, only occasionally giving a closed-mouth smile.

I wasn't being honest—with myself or with anyone in my life. And eventually, that dishonesty caught up with me and dragged me down.

Life is full of hard stuff. There's no way around it. But coping with hard stuff becomes less draining when you're honest about it. When you allow yourself to say, "This is hard." Just as I had with the chairs at the retreat. Recognizing the pain and struggles, giving them a name, sets you up to tackle them. You know they'll be tiring and challenging, so you ask for help, let yourself rest, give yourself grace. When you say to yourself, *This is hard*, you start to treat it like a hard thing—something that may require more than you can do alone.

Slumped over my washing machine in my laundry room, I finally allowed myself to say, "This is hard." And although I still had to do a lot of work and get a lot of help to haul myself out of depression, that one little truth made the battle ahead possible.

For the longest time, I described my dark days of depression as a period of my life when the lights went out. I now realize that it was the opposite. A light was turning on so that I would be able to see myself. Finally, I would come into view. And you know what? The things in my life that I thought disqualified me of being worthy turned out to be my qualifiers. I needed to experience firsthand love. An internal love that rises up like a wellspring of life, fully loving everything about my creation, embracing all my life experiences, good and bad, recognizing all that makes me the woman I am today. The kind of love that isn't looking for approval, validation, or permission to show up to the table as myself.

The journey to getting to this table required some reflection, looking back to understand that I can do hard things. After all, those hard things created the perfect recipe for who I am today.

Food for the Soul, One Dish at a Time

Let me introduce to you a vital part of my healing journey, something I believe will nourish your soul as we journey from chapter to chapter. As I stated in the introduction, this book will offer you both real and metaphorical ways to build your own table by showing you how I built my table with ingredients from my life, one dish at a time. Cooking saved my life. The kitchen became my sanctuary. God used cooking to turn the power back on inside my soul.

Whenever I can, I incorporate food into my coaching practice. It's an atmosphere shifter. When you take a seat at the table, your mind is prepared to be fed. I call it soul food therapy: for the mind, body, and soul. If I can get you to my table, I can change your life!

I've been privileged to sit at the feet of some of the best cooks in the world and become a classically trained chef myself. But you don't have to go to culinary school or apprentice with masters to take charge of your table. We're the master chefs of our own lives, and we acquire all the necessary ingredients as we matriculate through life. We have what it takes to create well-seasoned dishes for our tables.

The first recipe I'd like to share is a classic punch bowl. This nostalgic recipe brings me right back to twelve-year-old Tommi. It was a staple drink for our holiday and family celebrations.

It was also a centerpiece for a Nana Edie spread. She is the best chef I have ever met. It was inside her kitchen where I first unearthed a soul-stirring love for cooking legacy-inspired food. Like all of Nana Edie's food, this recipe is quick and straightforward. You dump all the ingredients into the punch bowl and get a tasty drink that mirrors a dessert. Although it's very simple and easy to make, it's filled with a variety of ingredients that come together to create something delicious. The ingredients are all enjoyable apart, but when they're combined, a new recipe comes to life. That is the story of my table!

At various seasons of my life, I couldn't imagine who I might become or how I might change. As I've matured and become well seasoned, I've realized that when I bring all my parts forward, a new version of myself is born. I get the opportunity to edit the measurements of the recipe so that when the ingredients come together, I experience love in every bite.

The classic punch bowl speaks to my personal mantra, "It's all good." Yes, life is hard, but it will all work together for my good. I just have to keep living!

Fruity Punch Bowl

INGREDIENTS:

1 quart fruit punch juice

2 liters ginger ale

1 bag frozen mixed fruit

½ gallon orange sherbet

INSTRUCTIONS:

In a punch bowl, add sherbet in the middle of the bowl and surround with fruit.

Pour in juice and then ginger ale.

Chapter Two

I'm Not Going to Make It

> And somehow, after everything, she still bloomed in the way she was meant to.
>
> —*Morgan Harper Nichols, All Along You Were Blooming: Thoughts for Boundless Living*

I'm pushing as hard as I can.

Even though my mom is rubbing my back—a familiar, soothing act she's done since I was a baby—it isn't dulling the excruciating pain. I squeeze my eyes shut and brace myself for the next contraction. I'm delirious from a Demerol injection. My butt has split open from front to back.

This is just way too hard!

Aside from the pain, all I can focus on is what the nurses and the doctor are thinking about me. The doctor's body language is downright cold. He stands by and refuses to do anything to comfort me. I avoid looking at the rest of the medical team in the delivery room and feel shame rising within me.

I'm a twelve-year-old girl in labor. A baby having a baby.

"I'm not going to make it!" I cry.

At twelve years old, I had no clue what was going to happen when my baby finally arrived. I had no clue what labor was about. The night before, when the pain started, my mom kept checking in with me.

"Are you feeling anything? Are you seeing anything in your panties when you're wiping yourself? Are you noticing any changes down there?"

I didn't know what the heck I was looking for! I wanted to say that to my mom in the most loving way possible. I had no clue what to expect. I was afraid. I was both excited and scared to have my baby.

Once the contractions started, they didn't stop. My mother and I lay down together on a twin mattress, and she rubbed my back. I was in too much pain to even register my fear. We stayed glued to that bed until it was time to go to the hospital.

Once there, my mother hovered over me nervously, her face etched in fear. The pain was making me cry and whine, shriek and howl. At one point, she slapped me. Hard. Knocking me out of the hysteria that was hijacking every fiber of my being. I cannot imagine how helpless my mom felt in that moment. My desperate wailing, sounds of utter defeat, rocked her to the core.

"Don't stop! Keep it up, Tommi!"

The commanding tone in her voice snapped me back to reality. I got the message: the only way my confusion, suffering, and shame would end was if I gave birth to the new life inside me.

I grabbed my knees and pushed with all my might.

My daughter Desiré was born with pecan brown skin, rosy

cheeks, and hair that looked like peach fuzz. I fell in love with her the second she was placed on my chest and looked at me inquisitively through swollen eyes and the signature torpedo head all five of my children would rock. I forgot all about the pain that had tortured my body just moments earlier.

I made it. Through sheer force of will and despite swearing that I couldn't.

Who Is in the Room with You?

Everyone's paths in life are different, but we all experience significant battles that force us to make tough decisions. We all face situations that cause us to doubt we'll make it through the storm.

Sometimes we require another voice to remind us, "You got this!" If my mom hadn't been there to encourage me to keep going, I truly don't know if I could have. There were many people in the room with me, but only one was speaking a language that breathed life into one of the hardest moments I needed to overcome. I didn't believe I could do it. That tough moment in my life serves as a consistent reminder that I can do hard things. And of the importance of being supported and supporting others.

It's worth considering who speaks into your life. Who are the people supporting you and holding you accountable on life's journey? Accountability also involves people calling you higher in life. Demanding that you become all you can be. They love you as you are but also encourage you to keep growing. Your circle of influencers contributes to how you view and do life. I constantly evaluate the people around me. It's my circle check. Are they in alignment with my personal desires? Do they take and not contribute? Am I a positive influence in their lives? Do they make me better and vice versa?

The older I've gotten, the more I recognize that the company I keep is not a casual matter. On the contrary, it's critically significant. It's not like following and liking strangers on social media. These are real people, intimately engaged in my life. Making it through hard things is not as hard when you have the right people supporting you through the storm. I had a baby and still had my family's love.

When Life Has Other Plans

Before I got pregnant, I was enrolled in a gifted and talented middle school. Not long after, I completed an application to attend an even more prestigious all-girls school. My childhood friend was afforded an opportunity to go, and I really hoped to do the same. In my case, resources were the barrier. Without a scholarship, it wasn't going to happen.

I remember the scholarship conversation between my mom, Nana Claudia, and myself like it was yesterday. We discussed the idea in Nana Claudia's sitting room. I was so excited. At that point, all I could see was my own potential as a bright young girl who could do big things.

Well, that was the extent of it: a hopeful conversation.

A few months later, I was pregnant.

Imagine having no vision for yourself, stuck viewing life through the lens of your situation. The whole world had decided that teenage pregnancy was a dead end. They were having congressional hearings about girls like me. It was an epidemic broadcast all over the news. There was an expected end for teenage mothers, and it didn't involve many of the aspirations I had for myself before I got pregnant.

Before, I was celebrated for my academic achievements. The

one picked to give speeches, selected for the city-wide orchestra playing cello, and chosen for special programming for standout students.

Afterward, the view of a bright future started to dim. My expectations settled to the bare minimum.

When it was time to go back to school after my daughter was born, everything was different. Instead of taking the long bus rides I was used to, I walked through an alley and around a corner to a local middle school that wasn't gifted, talented, all-girl, or prestigious. I never asked if I could return to the gifted and talented school. I assumed it was no longer an option. My mom told me that was where I was going to school, so that's where I went. It felt like I'd lost the right to express what I wanted, and everyone was doing me a favor by helping me get back on track. Because I'd left midyear, I had to start the seventh grade all over again. I was embarrassed.

As you can imagine, having a baby at twelve years old did not create an adult brain. My body had done adult stuff, but I was still immature in my thinking. My body grew in places it wasn't ready to do so. Along with that came a whole lot of stretch marks. My breasts had barely begun to form when they were prematurely traumatized! One long stretch mark, like a deflated balloon. I hated looking at myself in the mirror.

Thankfully, there was one area where I still shone: academics.

Game on.

The administration at my new school had provided a provisional plan that said if I excelled in the first semester, I would skip to the eighth grade. Well, I received straight A's on my report card and was in the eighth grade by the second semester. Doing well in academics made me feel normal and exceptional at the same time. I graduated from middle school as valedictorian and was feeling pretty good about myself. However, my life was quite a juxtaposition. On the one hand, I was proud of my academic success. On the other hand, I knew that rumors still swirled about me being a twelve-year-old girl with a baby. And I still felt the sting of shame. Although my parents didn't make me feel this way, I carried the weight of embarrassment I'd brought upon my family. To be clear, I wasn't ashamed of my baby girl. I was ashamed because I thought people viewed me as a bad girl for getting pregnant.

The Lens of Trauma

I did not have a vision for myself, and I quickly realized that no one else did either. I can't say that I blamed them. Despite my good grades, I was making many decisions that reflected the lack of vision I had for myself. My life was on a track headed straight to the welfare office and projects. Becoming valedictorian didn't change how I was perceived by others. I knew that. And it made my own self-image cloudy and confusing. It was a validating moment to receive recognition for my hard work, but I didn't know how to leverage that recognition into something more. I was a smart girl without a vision for my own possibilities; I had no clue that I could become whatever I wanted to be. I didn't connect the dots that I could use my smarts to go far in life.

Shame was my self-inflicted wound, and it had a heavy hand in obscuring my vision of who I was.

If you've experienced any form of trauma in your life, without exception, you know what shame feels like and how it affects the lens through which you view yourself. What do you see? Here's another way to ask that question: What are you looking at when you see yourself? For years, I viewed myself through my experiences, which were driving my personal narrative. I grew up in a town with a seven-mile radius. In my young mind, everybody knew everybody. After I had my daughter, I assumed that I was perceived as promiscuous or irresponsible by everyone, even strangers who didn't know my full story. This left me stuck between what they thought about me and what I thought about myself.

It was a diabolical combination. I found myself betraying my potential. I gave up on becoming great. Prior to getting pregnant, I aspired to attend a private school, win science fairs, and head off to college someday. I believed I had the faith of the people around me. After I had my daughter, I let all that go. It wasn't until I was older that I saw how this experience of shame shaped my vision of myself. It made me question my worthiness. Hard times were many, and I believed they were the consequences for my bad decisions. I thought I was getting what I deserved. It's hard to explain. I settled for doing the bare minimum because I thought my choices had sealed my fate—that there was a limit to how far I would go in life.

I had to free myself from this imagined, self-imposed mental prison.

I was stuck. I wish I had been mature enough to recognize that toxic thought cycles were tainting my vision so that I could have broken them! But my eyes were focused on the past. It became impossible to see the future. Because my past was in front of me. The past is a lesson that is part of life's curriculum. There are more lessons to come as long as we're blessed to keep living. In the meantime, I started acting out what I assumed people thought about me. My friends were much older than I was and with more experience in doing the wrong things. It was a group who accepted me and who didn't turn their noses up at me. Staying out late, drinking, smoking, among other harmful behaviors, had become my normal. Having a baby should have been the least of my concerns. That wouldn't hold me back; my behavior would. Although I could hide my toxic behavior, I couldn't hide that I had a baby. She became my saving grace.

Back then, people didn't talk about a future beyond teenage pregnancy. We must stop repeating the same lesson over and over. Just as in school, you learn the lesson purposefully designed to prepare you for the next. Even lessons derived from the consequences of choices resulting from others or yourself have the power to help us become better. Perspective is everything. I had no business having a baby at twelve years old, but I did. I wasn't mature enough to use the experience to grow. Being responsible for the life of another person is not a joke. I was no longer twelve-year-old Tommi playing with her doll babies. I was responsible for a real baby. In the sixth grade, I was late to school often. Many mornings I didn't feel like walking those few miles to school. After having my baby girl, my education should have been of the utmost importance. In the seventh grade, I went from being late in the sixth grade to having truancy issues. When the truancy officer knocked on my door, I would say, "I had to stay home to take care of my baby." That wasn't true. I would wait for my parents to leave for work and then sneak my friends over to play hooky from school. My parents didn't find out. At some point I became convicted. Looking at Desiré lying in her crib one evening, I thought, *What am I doing?*

Upon reflection, I now see that resilience became one of my staple ingredients in the maturation process. There were times when I had to self-correct my behavior. My parents worked. They trusted my siblings and me to handle the things we were responsible for. This was nothing out of the ordinary for the many latchkey kids with working parents. Surviving hard things as a child was commonplace for me, so I took for granted what it required for me to survive. Self-accountability, love, and discipline help us improve, heal, and readjust negative thoughts or perspectives.

The truth helps!

That's why it's important to take regular inventory of and pay attention to the tools available for us to pick up along our journey. I know that my parents weren't excited to get up early every day to go to work, sometimes working triple or double shifts, but they did it anyway. I learned early to correct my choices but not because I always wanted to. I had to. My daughter was a constant reminder, even when I wanted to be a "normal" kid. We need these to cultivate, nurture, shape, apply, refine, deconstruct, and rebuild ourselves when life requires next-level strengths, wisdom, vision, knowledge, and skills to be used at our next crossroads moment.

Getting to the bottom of patterns and taking the empowered step of removing the tainted lens is something you're more than capable of doing. Even when you feel like you can't, you can.

Remember, it's *your life*.

Life is not happening to you; it's happening for you.

Looking back, I know that the day I gave birth to my daughter was the day that I began my journey. My life was forever changed. I understood that there was a lot of life left for me to live.

I didn't think I was going to make it, but I did.

Food for the Soul, One Dish at a Time

My mom knocked that determination back into me. When I'm in my kitchen, my sanctuary, I always think about my mom making deviled eggs. She made the best deviled eggs. She taught me my first legacy-inspired recipe to be served at a special occasion. When considering the lesson I learned from this dish, my mom's resiliency comes to mind. Like all of us, my mom has a story. She managed life in a way that was necessary for her to survive. Like an egg, my mom had built a hard shell on the outside to protect what was on the inside.

I realize today that my mom was teaching me to create that shell of protection to guard what was on the inside of me. However, as I matured, I also learned that you can't access the goodness on the inside unless you break the shell open.

Deviled Eggs *with* Candied Bacon

INGREDIENTS:

6 eggs

4 cups cold water

3 tablespoons mayonnaise

3 generous dashes hot sauce

¾ teaspoon sugar

¼ teaspoon salt

Pinch of pepper

Paprika for garnish

Candied bacon for garnish (see next page)

Chopped chives for garnish

INSTRUCTIONS:

Place eggs in a medium saucepan. Pour in the water. Bring to a boil for approximately 5 to 7 minutes.

After the water comes to a boil, lower the heat so that the water reduces to a simmer. Allow the eggs to simmer for 12 minutes.

Crack the eggshells and peel under cool running water. Dry the eggs with a paper towel. Slice the eggs lengthwise. Remove the yolks and place in a medium bowl. Place the egg whites on a serving platter.

Use the back of a fork to mash the yolks into a fine crumble, then add the mayonnaise, hot sauce, sugar, salt, and pepper. Mix well. Alternatively, place yolks, mayonnaise, hot sauce, sugar, salt, and pepper in a medium bowl. Combine with a hand mixer until smooth.

Evenly distribute a heaping spoonful of the mixture into the egg whites. Garnish with a sprinkle of paprika, bacon crumbles, and chives.

Candied Bacon

INGREDIENTS:

12 slices of uncured bacon

Pinch of cayenne pepper

1/3 cup brown sugar

INSTRUCTIONS:

Preheat the oven to 350°F. Line a baking sheet with aluminum foil or parchment paper. Place the bacon strips on the pan.

In a small bowl, mix the cayenne pepper and brown sugar. Evenly sprinkle over the bacon slices. Bake in the oven on the middle rack for 15 to 20 minutes.

Remove from the oven. Allow bacon to cool on the pan for 2 minutes and transfer the slices to a wire cooling rack. Make sure the bacon slices are not touching one another.

After the bacon cools and crisps up, take a couple of slices and break into bite-size pieces. Use for deviled egg garnish. Use the leftover slices for a salad fixing, sandwich topper, or simply enjoy as a sweet and spicy snack.

Chapter Three

How Did I Get Here?

> Unfortunately, my history is a familiar tale to so many reading this. I just wish I could go back and talk to that young girl that I was. What would I say? It is not your fault.
>
> *—Valarie, survivor of domestic abuse*

There's something comforting about the heat blasting out of the vents, pajamas, and cozy slippers while looking out the window at the leaves rustling in the cold winter air. This was the best day ever! Just weeks earlier I'd sent my Christmas list to Santa asking for a red boom box with a yellow microphone that I'd seen in the Sears catalog, and now here I was sitting on my bedroom floor with this amazing gift, singing and playing and having the time of my three-year-old life.

I opened my mouth to belt out *jingle bells, jingle bells* when—boom! My bedroom door flew open. My eyes shifted from looking at my brand-new toy to a relative of mine who was naked and had blood covering her face. Our rapid heartbeats seemed to be in sync. We didn't say a word. She jumped behind my door, keeping her eyes on its wooden back side. My gaze stayed fixed on her, waiting for her to glance back at me.

My body froze, butt glued to the floor. So many thoughts raced through my mind. I was both curious and afraid. I heard police sirens and squad cars pull up outside. With no explanation, I was left to narrate the situation in my little mind, filling in the details to create the full picture of what had happened.

You may remember that I hinted at this story in the introduction to this book. As I mentioned then, my takeaway of the day was that a man—who was a regular part of my family life and very kind to me—loved my relative and had hurt her badly. She was trembling for her life. I had no idea where everyone else was. In that moment, the world paused. One minute she was behind my door, and the next she was gone. Where she went, I also have no idea. The memories that remain are patchy. The things I remember most clearly are the ones I can palpably feel, like they just happened.

Three-year-old me looked out my window and saw the police walking the man who'd hurt my relative to the patrol car, his hands cuffed behind his back. The officer pushed down the man's bald head so that it wouldn't hit the doorframe as he climbed into the back seat.

We lived in an apartment complex, and anytime there was the slightest bit of commotion, everyone came outside to see what was going on. As soon as the police car pulled away, everyone went back inside their homes. That was the end. The world came off pause, and it was back to the regularly scheduled program. No discussion from anyone. I don't even know if my parents knew what I had witnessed.

Later that day, I was outside playing with my cousins. Just hours after beating my relative to the point of bleeding, the bald man approached from out of nowhere. He'd left with the police and returned by himself. Our giggles halted, and just like in a movie, everything moved in slow motion—his long strides and heavy footsteps as he walked toward the apartment and the sweat running down his shiny bald head. I wasn't afraid because he'd always been very kind to me, but I remember thinking, *He's back*, and wondering what that meant to my relative. Would he hurt her again?

The next day, I saw the bald man and my relative together, laughing and embracing as if nothing had happened. *This was normal*, I thought. This was love.

Even when I was little, I knew that the families who lived around me were doing the best they could. There wasn't a lot of time for conversation because people were busy working to take care of their families. My parents weren't exempt. They had to provide for our family. Which meant you learned how to live life by watching people do life.

That day my relative came to our home next door for safety, I remember hearing her say, "He's still in there" as she made her way up our steps. My parents were providing for my siblings and me but also protecting her. That day I decided that was what love looked and felt like. That was love. It was very clear to me. The harm my relative encountered. The care and compassion my parents gave her. The embrace the bald man and my relative shared shortly after. I felt all of it. I saw all of it. That combination became my definition of love.

The Cycle of Abuse

So at thirteen years old, when a boy who'd professed his love for me smacked the living daylights out of me, I thought, *He must really love me.* I believed harm and love were synonymous, holding on to the definition of love I'd created at three years old. And when I found myself in a three-year abusive relationship with this boy, from ninth through twelfth grades, it made sense in terms of how I defined love.

The smacks turned into closed-fist beatdowns until I was literally on the ground. Black eyes and bruised ribs became normal. I had mastered hiding my bruises with side bangs draped over my eye, makeup, and clothing. *Still,* I told myself, *this was normal.* This was how a woman in love was supposed to act.

One day I came home from school to find all my clothes thrown out of my own house and onto the front porch. My boyfriend had become angry that day in school because I was hanging with my friends instead of with him. He left early and, to my dismay, had gone to my home. He knew he could climb the tree outside and get high enough to enter my second-story bedroom window, which is what he did. He trashed my room . . . but that's not all he did.

Seconds after I opened the front door, he bum-rushed me before I could enter. He was armed with a pair of rusty steel scissors from our kitchen. The cocktail of fear and desperation that flooded me before each beating rushed through every fiber of my being.

His voice full of wicked glee, he shouted, "If you're ugly, no one will want you."

He pushed me down to the ground, took the scissors, and started cutting the front of my hair.

"Look at you. Ugly. No one will want you."

I sobbed as I lay on the ground. I knew it wasn't over. I balled up to protect my face, but not for the reasons you think. I covered my face so that there would be no evidence of the beating I was about to get because I didn't want *him* to get in trouble.

He snatched my gold shell earrings out of my ears and stomped on them.

"You think you cute. Not no more."

Buying those earrings had been such an accomplishment for me. At the time, I was working on Joe Brown's ice-cream truck making fifty dollars a day. I'd seen those earrings and had fallen in love with them but couldn't pay for them all at once. So I went to Philly to put them on layaway with twenty dollars, hoping to get to the full price of eighty dollars as quickly as I could manage. I traveled back and forth on the train, putting down ten-dollar deposits, paying down the layaway a little at a time, until they were paid off. I was so proud of myself. I didn't have those earrings for a week before he destroyed them.

I wished that love didn't have to hurt so badly. My three-year-old definition of love was truer than ever.

On the Bridge

This type of thing happened more times than I care to remember. Physical, verbal, and mental abuse on repeat. All validating my definition of love. We had developed a reputation among our friends for being this way. Every time we went out, we'd get into a fight. They were sick of it. Our final outing would be no different.

One evening, he and I went to a comedy show at the War Memorial in Trenton, New Jersey, with another couple. In hindsight, I should have known the type of night I was in for because he'd made fun of my clothes and told me my breath stank, berating me with put-down after put-down. Constantly taking shots that caused me to shrink down to nothing. Then again, nothing could have prepared me for what would happen that night.

We left the comedy show and walked back to the west side of town. As the walk progressed, so did his abuse. He started smacking me on the back of the head. By then, our friends had had it with us.

My friend said, "That's why I hate going out with y'all. All you do is fight!"

But we continued, with him hitting me and me hitting him back. As we approached the Calhoun Street bridge, the fight escalated further until finally my girlfriend shouted, "Stop it!"

In response to this, he scooped me up and hoisted me in the air with Incredible Hulk–like strength to throw me over the bridge. I looked down to see concrete and broken glass one hundred feet below. My sixteen years of life flashed before my eyes. It was a moment out of a movie.

I cried out to my friend, "Call my mom!"

This was a breakthrough moment for me. Finally, I was willing to get him in trouble! Up until that point, I'd done everything in my power to protect him. To protect us. But as he held me in the air, threatening to let go, I no longer cared about protecting him. I wanted to save *myself.*

A grave feeling began to overtake my body. It reminded me of another time in my life—giving birth to Desiré—when I didn't think I was going to make it.

I'm not going to make it! I cried once again, this time silently to myself.

Then I started having a conversation with God in my head.

Please save me, I thought.

Instantly, God gave me the words I needed to negotiate my way down to the ground. I professed my love for my abuser. I told him we needed to stop before something happened that we would both regret. The words bought time for him to cool off and come back to himself. He put me down.

My shirt was practically ripped all the way off my body. I gripped it closed as we finished walking the longest three blocks of my life. I kept repeating to myself, *We just need to make it to his house*. As we approached it, I told him I was going to keep going to my house so that we could have some time to calm down. To my surprise, he agreed. I don't know this for a fact, but I think he scared himself. There was a stillness about his demeanor that I hadn't seen after any of the other beatings. He had almost killed me. There was no turning back from that for either of us.

A Violent End

I didn't speak to him for two weeks following the bridge incident. Nor did I share the details with anyone else. When I walked away from him that night, I knew I would never go back. It was a little strange that he didn't reach out to me or show up at my house, and I started to worry about what he might do next. My suspicions were correct. One day my doorbell rang just before I was headed out to work at Mercer Hospital. The same hospital where I had given birth to Desiré. It was him. Home alone, immediately my mind flashed back to the bridge. He was acting weird, and I was deathly afraid. He was sweaty and wouldn't look at me.

I didn't open the door right away. My friend was on her way to drive me to work. She arrived and saw him on my porch. When she walked up, I opened the door for her. He pushed past me, went upstairs, and shut himself in my bathroom.

This can't be good, I thought.

My heart started pounding in my chest. Fear consumed me from my head down to my toes. It was imperative that he leave my house immediately. I was going to be late for work, which just added to my stress. I banged on the door as hard as I could and said, "Come out of there."

He didn't respond immediately but eventually came out and walked right past me down the steps, positioning himself by the front door. I ran down the steps to leave, and he tried to prevent me by gripping my arm as tightly as he could. I managed to break away and jumped in my friend's car. As we drove off, he pursued on foot, kicking the back bumper when he realized we weren't stopping.

When we got to the corner, I saw my dad exiting off the highway. Instead of taking me to work, I asked my friend to turn the car around and go back to my house so that I could tell my dad what had happened. At this point, I no longer cared about being late for work. I was scared out of my mind and wanted to live. The boy had pulled off in his own car before my dad had parked. My friend and I jumped out of the car, talking a mile a minute, sharing the details about what had happened. My dad listened, got us inside, then went upstairs to check the bathroom.

He found an empty bottle of Excedrin in the bathroom sink.

I immediately informed his mom about the situation, then from that point on discontinued my relationship with him.

I've shared this story on numerous occasions in my work as an adult advocating to end domestic violence. The part of the story I don't discuss is that I was pregnant the night he tried to kill me. I carried the burden of shame of staying in an abusive relationship and convincing myself that it was love. But that night on the bridge, my light did not go out. I lived to see another day.

In fact, my light turned on in that moment, and I could see myself. The image was crystal clear. Before, I'd lived every day scared for my life as each beating escalated and became more violent. The fear was part of my reality, and I never considered walking away. My plan was to have the baby, graduate high school, get an apartment, and live happily ever after with my abuser. How does someone getting their brains beaten out believe that they're living the dream? Easily. Abuse had penetrated my mind so deeply that I was delusional, thinking my real-life nightmare was somehow a dream come true. But after the night on the bridge, I saw things differently. I made the decision that I wanted to live a life free of my abuser. All the things that would keep me tethered to him had to be released.

I woke the next morning and shared two things with my mom: I wanted to have an abortion, and I wanted to go to college. The power of this moment was in my courage to choose myself. Please try not to read this part of my story through the lens of your own beliefs. Read it and be proud of my decision to break a cycle of destruction. The truth of the matter is that my decision on that day saved me from self-destruction. Settling for a subpar existence filled with a warped definition of love led me to not love myself.

Real love does not hurt intentionally.

The Tides Finally Change

You may be wondering how those pivotal decisions affected my life. I got an abortion and enrolled at Temple University. My SAT scores were trash, so I needed a miracle to get into school. My cousin worked in admissions and pulled some strings to make it happen. My mom was a newly licensed real estate agent and used the proceeds from her first transaction to pay for my first semester of college. Although I didn't see the full picture of how valuable I was, others around me hadn't given up on me. They continued to believe in me while I began the journey of finding my way to myself.

Oh, and I connected with my husband-to-be, Troy, within a month after I started classes. My time at Temple may have started out a little rough, but it quickly became a welcoming new season for me.

Thinking about this moment of my life fills my heart with a tremendous amount of gratitude. It's not lost on me that the day on the bridge could have been the last chapter of my life. I reflect on it often to remind myself that I'm still here for a reason. I negotiated with a boy who didn't see the value of my life. I fought to live.

For every opportunity I get to extend grace, empathy, and compassion to others—to provide them with a chance to grow into the life they've been given—I do it. In exchange, I ask them to do the same for themselves and for others. Life is hard. Hard takes wisdom to navigate. Wisdom is acquired by living through difficult times and benefiting from the experience of others who have successfully survived those tough moments in life.

Success doesn't always equate to doing everything right. Some of the most valuable experiences come from doing things wrong and learning from our mistakes. Our lives are the sum of our many experiences. This was mine.

My story has positively influenced many domestic violence survivors and young women who find themselves at a crossroads.

After several years of not talking about what had happened to me in my abusive relationship, courage knocked on my door. I began sharing my story across the nation, committed to normalizing the conversation, not the behavior. I'm a thriving survivor advocating to end domestic violence.

Food for the Soul, One Dish at a Time

Life lessons add dishes to our table. Dishes that invoke gratitude. The next dish for our table is potato salad. Before you compose this dish, you must transform the original state of the ingredients for them to be successful in the end. What if no one told you that you needed to cook the potatoes and eggs? What if you put a whole onion in the bowl without dicing it first? The result would be something completely different.

Sometimes we benefit from the counsel others give us along the way. Other times we figure it out ourselves through trial and error. Occasionally, we keep doing it wrong because it's the only way we know how. I believe in sharing my experience so that you can get this potato salad right!

You boil, peel, and dice the eggs. You dice and boil the potatoes. You dice the onions. It may seem like a lot, but there's no way of completing the recipe without working your way through the process of preparation. My dice may look different from yours. You may overcook your potatoes. It's all good.

The required ingredients to make the potato salad are all basics that most of us have in our refrigerators and pantries. If you need an ingredient you don't have, ask someone if you may use some of theirs. To start the cooking process for any recipe, you need to understand the ingredients to determine the best way to prep them. This particular dish is full of ingredients produced in the gardens of our lives, with a few here and there gifted from someone else.

A truthful conversation provides understanding so that you can start the process of creating the best recipe for *your* life.

Smashed Red Potato Salad

INGREDIENTS:

3 pounds red potatoes, medium diced

3 boiled eggs, peeled and chopped

¼ cup onion, small diced

1 cup mayonnaise

½ cup relish

1 teaspoon celery seeds

3 tablespoons sugar

1½ teaspoons salt

½ teaspoon black pepper

Paprika for garnish (optional)

INSTRUCTIONS:

Boil potatoes and eggs in a large pot for approximately 12 minutes. The timer starts once the water begins boiling. Cook until the potatoes are fork tender.

Drain in a strainer and rinse with cool water.

Remove the eggs and peel. Allow potatoes and eggs to cool.

In a large bowl, add half of the potatoes and smash with a potato masher or with the back of a fork. Add remaining potatoes, chopped eggs, and remaining ingredients. Mix until ingredients are well combined.

Spoon potato salad into a serving dish and garnish with paprika. Cover and refrigerate for 30 minutes.

Chapter Four

The Truth Helps

> To be yourself in a world that is constantly trying to make someone else is the greatest accomplishment.
>
> —*Ralph Waldo Emerson, Essays*

I made it to college! Now what was I going to do with myself?

I had spent most of my high school days getting high, skipping class, and totally disengaging from academics. Now I was at Temple University—financed by my mom's $10,000 investment from her first home sale—only to find myself floundering like a fish out of water. Although my surroundings had changed, my thoughts about myself had not, and I realized I was comparing myself to my peers. They discussed their goals with their academic advisers, consulted one another on class selections, and formed study groups. I felt like I was in a foreign country where everyone was speaking a different language.

I had made the decision to attend college, and my mom had used every bit of her money to get me to Temple. After all that, I was terrified that I would fail miserably because I didn't believe I was qualified enough to succeed. I didn't believe I was worthy, which meant it was easy for me to not try.

I knew college was a way forward; that's why I wanted to go in the first place. But I was convinced that I would fail before I had a chance to find out if I could even be successful. An abusive relationship leaves invisible mental wounds that the human eye cannot see, and my wounds ran deep.

I wasn't healed simply because I had taken a step in the right direction, however difficult it had been. That step was incredibly important and would become the moment I reflect back on to remind myself of how strong and courageous I am. To remember that I'm a survivor.

But during my time at Temple, I had no idea that my struggles to succeed in school were related to the abuse I had endured. I didn't know that the voice inside telling me I couldn't do anything right was the haunting echo of my abuser. The only way I knew to hold the voice at bay was to keep walking straight ahead, blindly but steadily.

The Turning Point

One day as I prepared to make an attempt at my coursework, I reflected on the time previously mentioned when I received the honor of valedictorian of my ninth-grade class. It was enough of a reminder that it was possible for me to be successful in college. I chose to put forth real effort and gave it another shot with an upcoming chemistry exam. I cracked open the book, read the chapter, and completed the study guide. I reviewed the notes from lectures right before walking into the classroom where I had spent more time asleep with my head on the desk than listening.

But I had prepared for this test and showed up with confidence for the first time since beginning college.

I nervously awaited the results for two long days. When it was time to check the wall outside the lecture hall to get my test score, I was incredibly nervous. Sweating in anticipation. I walked up to the list of grades and moved my finger with trepidation down the paper to where my name was listed.

Wow. I got a seventy-four.

Now a seventy-four was a far cry from the straight A's I'd earned during my middle school career, crowned with the distinct honor of being named valedictorian, but from where my feet stood in this season of my life, I was elated. Although it wasn't reflected on my facial expression, my heart was smiling big on the inside.

Sometimes we must demonstrate to ourselves that we can do hard things. This requires effort on our part. I truly believed that I couldn't be successful in college. I told myself repeatedly that my life wouldn't amount to anything. Circumstances had beaten the life out of me. My choices were choosing for me. But even though I had made many poor decisions, there was enough evidence that I was capable of so much more. And that helped me take tiny steps toward change.

A personal exercise I do even now when I believe that I can't accomplish something is to ask God to show me a time when I demonstrated that I could. That I was capable of doing hard things. An example of this is when I had to write a paper for Sociology 101. I was completely overwhelmed to the point that I didn't want to try. When I looked for evidence of my ability to successfully conquer this assignment, I remembered the time I wrote a paper in the eighth grade and got an A+. My teacher used my paper as an example for all of her classes to illustrate what she was looking for in the assignment. This memory helped me remember that the ability to write great papers lived inside me.

There were a few times at Temple when I chose to put in the work and try my best. Most of the time, though, I felt like I was in a boat all alone, trying desperately to paddle upstream against a strong, merciless current.

Meeting My Match

Academics were a struggle, but other aspects of my life at Temple brought me a lot of joy. In the process of navigating college life, I connected with Troy, and we had a beautiful romance that became a great escape from the challenging obstacles I was experiencing in my classes.

Troy and I had both grown up in Trenton, so we had common friends. My sister's husband at that time was the one who introduced us. I had never encountered a boy who was kind and thoughtful like him. He was raised by his grandparents. Maybe that explained his gentlemanly qualities and old soul.

On top of my academic challenges, I felt a lot of guilt about being away from my daughter. But Troy curated a divine place in the midst of my uncertainty. He would send me dozens of roses weekly. We would talk through the night until it was time to wake up the next morning. It was a storybook fairy tale, but it was real.

Revisiting My Love of Softball

When I was apart from Troy, I was still making choices detrimental to the world I desired to create. Although my marijuana usage was getting the better of me, I decided to try out for the Temple softball team. I had been an outstanding third baseman in high school before having a temper tantrum and quitting the team.

I didn't have the self-knowledge to recognize this in either high school or college, but I struggled to respond to challenges rationally during my teenage years. My mind immediately shifted to confrontation anytime I thought that I was being challenged. I felt a strong need to defend myself: the abuse I had endured conditioned me to be prepared to fight.

And that wasn't all. In my abusive relationship, I was constantly trying to control the situation, steering things toward the outcome of not being physically harmed. Storming away from my high school coaches was my way of controlling the situation. Again, I knew this only in retrospect. But at the time, I could still tell that finding a way to play again would be healing for me. If I could make the Temple softball team, I could get back something I had loved since the third grade.

When the Temple softball coach mentioned that we would have to pass a drug test, I panicked. I remember watching a family member drinking vinegar to flush their system out to pass a drug test for work. *Surely this would work for me*, I thought. I drank an entire bottle of apple cider vinegar. I still get nauseous just thinking about it. At this point, my dad had proudly sold T-shirts as a fundraiser for the team, so I had to pass that drug test by any means necessary.

But before I had the opportunity to test, I chickened out. I was terrified that I would fail and disappoint my coach and my parents (again). It was too much to bear. I went to the coach's office to tell her I was stepping away from the team to focus on my academics. She tried to convince me to stick with it. I declined and walked down the hallway feeling unworthy once again.

Leading a Double Life

At that point, I started to notice that my feelings of unworthiness showed up in direct correlation to my personal decisions. Smoking marijuana was my choice to make and my choice to own. Why did I continue to sabotage my opportunities to move toward a better life? On the one hand, I had this beautiful storybook romance blossoming with Troy. On the other hand, I was continuing to do more of the same destructive stuff and producing the same ragged results. Entering into a relationship with a wonderful person could change my behavior. I knew this. It could influence better choices, but it was on me to make better life decisions.

Early on in my relationship with Troy, I still was drinking and smoking. God knows I would never do it around him! My homegirls were a different story. One time, my friends and I got high in our dorm room. With a shower cap positioned over the smoke detector and a towel placed over the crack at the bottom of the door, we were having a good time. Our giggles swiftly shifted to panic when our resident assistant started knocking on the door. We made up a story that the smell was a new incense we were trying out, but he didn't believe us. We got busted.

Instantly, we sobered up. Our punishment was creating "Don't Do Drugs" posters to hang around the dorm, plus probation. I was mortified and so ashamed. Imagining Troy finding out made my stomach hurt. He was straitlaced, no drugs or alcohol. Living a dual life was exhausting.

Just like I learned how to love at three years old by watching my relatives endure abuse, I learned how to live by watching the people around me scrape by as best they could. I saw them living with disappointment, self-soothing with substances, looking for love in all the wrong places, and settling for second best or worse. Those choices and behaviors became my blueprint for living.

But after the incident in the dorm, I began to see things another way. I realized that to change my behavior, I needed to change how I perceived myself.

I love the quote by Lao Tzu: "The journey of a thousand miles begins with a single step." At Temple, I didn't quite know where I was going, but I knew I needed to course-correct. If I didn't pursue an intimate relationship with myself, I could lose my relationship with Troy. He made it clear that he wasn't interested in drugs. He and I had been exposed to many of the same things growing up. They'd had devastating effects on our families and community. He'd chosen to run far away from it while I had chosen to run toward it. Troy didn't explicitly tell me that my smoking and drinking were a deal-breaker, but he didn't need to. His personal convictions spoke for him.

I wasn't willing to lose the love of my life because I didn't know how to love myself. I had to figure this out.

Changing the Story

There are many reasons why we might become bystanders in our own lives. My reason was shame: My relationship with shame intensified after my abusive relationship, leading to what I termed firsthand abuse. I became harder on myself than ever before. I wasn't proud of having figured out how to get out of an abusive relationship; it was embarrassing to me to have been in one in the first place. My self-talk was toxic, eating away at my soul. The damaging words rang loudly, drowning out the truth that it wasn't my fault.

I wasn't ashamed of the abusive relationship itself. I was

ashamed because I thought people viewed me as stupid for being part of the relationship, for not getting out sooner.

My shame was fueled by what I believed others thought about me.

I vividly remember thinking that my relationship with Troy wouldn't last. It all felt too good to be true. He was kind, thoughtful, and loving in a way I had never experienced. It was like I was trying to talk my way out of happiness. It also didn't help that many people had advised Troy not to date me because I was fast. That's what they said about teenage moms. It left an asterisk in my mind that one day he would take their advice. I moved through the beginning of our courtship holding my breath and waiting for that day to come.

He didn't flinch. I didn't feel judged by him. This may sound strange, but his lack of judgment was extremely uncomfortable. I didn't understand how he could look past the scarlet letter that others had marked me with. But he saw my value before I realized the value in myself. Troy wasn't going anywhere. Something inside told me to grab hold of him and never let go. This was the beginning of my journey toward self-discovery.

It was time to snatch the pen, time to write my own recipe for happiness.

To this day I refer to Troy as my person. We should all be so fortunate to have a person or people who usher us along until the cylinders click and the gears start moving in our minds. I will admit that this wasn't easy, even though my connection to Troy was so strong from the start. Even though I knew he was my person. It always felt like I had a dirty little secret, because in the deepest parts of my being, I didn't understand how he could love someone like me. The fact that he saw me and loved all of me was initially difficult to accept. The battle was always me versus me. I sure am glad I won!

As strange as it felt at first, Troy's belief in me eventually helped me start believing in myself. And his example of living without alcohol or drugs inspired me. So I took the leap forward toward hope, toward a future better than I could ever have imagined for myself. It was a surreal time that ignited my confidence and unleashed my sense of value. In that moment, I turned the page on my chapter of despair. I started to believe that the ending of my story had the potential to be uplifting. It could turn out like the storylines I used to give to my Barbies as a kid. A real-life happy ending.

If you're wondering whether I finished my degree at Temple University, I did not. In my second year, Troy sustained a knee injury, and I left school to care for him. He was in his rookie year of the National Football League playing for the Miami Dolphins, and I'd seen the injury take place on live television. I woke early the next morning to call him. This was before cell phones, so I called him collect from the pay phone in the lobby of my dormitory. Without hesitation, I asked if he wanted me to come to Fort Lauderdale to care for him. It was the least I could do—an opportunity to return the kindness, thoughtfulness, and love Troy showered upon me. He made my reservation, and off to the friendly skies I went.

I thought the assignment was simple: Go take care of Troy. Little did I know that my life was about to change forever. In ways I couldn't imagine.

Food for the Soul, One Dish at a Time

The dishes are beginning to fill our table. This one may seem too plain to include. After all, the recipe is a simple ratio. But when you have the right amount of this and the right amount of that, the ingredients come together to make exactly what you desire. The key is to know the formula.

When I first attempted to make rice, I had to try several times before it turned out right. I was using a tried-and-tested skill to complete a new endeavor, but I realized that it required a different approach. My "dump" cook approach resulted in several failed attempts that led to undercooked or overcooked nonpalatable rice. That approach wasn't appropriate for making perfect, fluffy rice.

Rice has a simple ratio of one part rice to two parts water that will turn out perfectly every time, and it's found in the directions listed on the rice packaging. Although my invaluable tool of knowing when to add a touch of this or a pinch of that serves me well in many of life's challenges, knowing when to resort to a by-the-book, proven approach is a necessary discipline. There's no need to make life more difficult.

When I think of white rice, it brings my Nana Claudia to mind. There was always a side of white rice at her dinner table. We served ourselves from the pots on the stove. It was at your discretion how much rice went onto your plate and what you added to enhance the flavor of an otherwise bland dish. My go-tos were the pan drippings from the meat she prepared. I can still smell and taste her food like it was yesterday.

Rice is a great example of a simple dish that can be transformed by adding an accompaniment of seasoning to the cooking process, mixing in other ingredients, or topping it with other flavors. Some of us operate better with a simple formula that will yield consistent results each and every time. The key is to not limit the possibilities. Start with the formula and take it to the next level by adding enhancements.

Rice does not have to be bland, and neither do you. Add the seasoning to your life that moves you beyond basic living to living boldly and full of flavor.

White Rice

INGREDIENTS:

1 cup white rice

2 cups tap water

Salt

INSTRUCTIONS:

Rinse the rice.

Use the right ratio of water. Add two parts water and one part rice to a large pot.

Bring the water to a boil. Once boiling, add a pinch of salt.

Reduce the heat to low, cover the pot, and maintain a gentle simmer. Do *not* remove the lid!

Cook until the water is absorbed, usually 15 to 18 minutes.

Once it's fully cooked, turn off the heat and let the rice sit, covered but off the burner, for about 10 minutes. During this time, the rice will get even fluffier as it steams.

Fluff the rice with a fork.

Chapter Five

The Bridge to Better

> Never to forget where we came from and always praise the bridges that carried us over.
>
> —Fannie Lou Hamer

We should always be on the lookout for bridges. A bridge is our opportunity to hope for something better. We may not know what's waiting for us on the other side, but when we allow our hearts to believe that there's an opportunity for something better, all we have to do is walk by faith. Life can change in an instant. One decision can be the beginning of a better life. One hopeful step onto a bridge can bring transformation.

From the very beginning, I was grateful that I took a walk of faith to go where Troy was leading. Honestly, it felt more like a beckoning to come higher. And as I made my way to Fort Lauderdale to be by his side through his recovery, US Airways literally took me to a higher altitude. When I touched down and walked the jet bridge, I knew I was crossing a bridge that put me on course to become a better me, both spiritually and mentally. My fate did not get walled off by the judgments of those who counted me out. Had I focused on the choir of people who murmured about me having a daughter or not being good enough for Troy, I may not have walked down that jet bridge. Thank God love had the power to take me higher! The path before me was paved with Troy's love, care, and affirmation in the sunshine state of Florida.

As I poured myself into comforting and caring for Troy while he rehabbed his season-ending knee injury, I found myself thinking about the times in my childhood when I felt most comforted myself. This is what is so beautiful about bridges: If you protect them, they let you go back and revisit the best parts of life again and again. My strongest memories of comfort involved my Nana Edie and my Nana Claudia preparing meals to soothe the troubles away.

Sick Days at Nana Claudia's

I will never forget this one morning on a school day when I woke up coughing. My mom peeked her head in the door and said, "If you cough one more time, you're staying home and going to your Nana Claudia's." I loved going to Nana Claudia's on sick days because she made me bologna sandwiches with a thin layer of mayonnaise and a few dots of yellow mustard on Wonder Bread that was cut into perfect triangles. So I coughed on purpose! My mom packed me into the Volkswagen van, and as we pulled into my Nana Claudia's driveway, I saw that she was standing at the screen door waiting for me. With bright eyes and a smirk on my face, I moseyed my way up the green-turf-carpeted porch steps and went into the house.

It wasn't even 8:00 a.m., and she had already finished her daily chores. The carpet lines were meticulously patterned, the plastic-covered furniture had been wiped down, and the bathroom was sparkling clean. I could smell the Pine-Sol in the air. This was going to be a great sick day, eating my bologna sandwiches, watching *The Price Is Right*, *The Young and the Restless*, *The Bold and the Beautiful*, *One Life to Live*, and *General Hospital* propped up on the couch next to my Nana Claudia! One day at her house was all it took. I was always magically better and ready to go to school the next day.

As I got older, I started to pay attention to how my grandmothers nourished and loved us through food. My greatest inspiration in the kitchen was my Nana Edie. She was special! She was a master at preparing food that healed the soul, not to mention that it was the best-tasting food I have had in my life. Her pot collection filled the musty basement, crowding onto makeshift shelves that my uncle had built. Her kitchen was a chef's dream. As a kid, I had no clue about brands like Wolf and Sub-Zero. Apparently, my Nana Edie did. Her gas stove had six burners, a griddle, and a side-by-side double oven adorned with Wolf's iconic red knobs. She had a huge Sub-Zero refrigerator and a butcher-block countertop.

My favorite place in the kitchen was seated at the round wooden table, with its claw feet and a hodgepodge of chairs surrounding it, positioned right in front of the woodburning fireplace. I tried pig-ear soup at that table! The only reason I ate it is because Nana Edie made it. The fireplace was snap, crackle, popping in one ear, and she was encouraging me to try it in the other. To my surprise, it tasted amazing. That was the first and last time I tried pig-ear soup. I'm convinced the soup was delicious because she filled the pot with her signature ingredient—love. As a kid, everything in my Nana Edie's kitchen felt huge to me, including her big heart that loved and cared for everyone who took a seat at her table.

Cooking Is Healing

These memories comforted me during this period of my life, caring for Troy as he recovered. And I definitely needed comfort because I was making huge changes—changes that scared me. Even though I was actively pushing aside all the negativity and judgment around my relationship with Troy, I was still only eighteen. I had been through a lot, but I was very young and very inexperienced. Everything was so new. Troy had a fully formed life, a home, a job playing for the Dolphins. He was in his rookie season, having a phenomenal season playing football, and he had injured himself. Would it be a career-ending injury? Would his life change forever—and mine along with it? What was I supposed to do with all these huge adult decisions? I felt like I was stepping into this role as a woman for the first time in my life, and I wasn't sure I was ready.

But I knew for sure that I needed to get to Florida, to make sure he was OK, and to show up for him in the way that he had shown up for me. He was hurt and worried about his future. And I was certain that I should be by his side while he recovered.

So there was fear connected to my journey across this bridge. I was afraid but did it anyway, because, in my heart, I believed there was something better on the other side.

By the time I was settled in Troy's house in Florida, I knew I'd made the right choice. He needed loving to help him heal! The kind that was stirred up in Nana Edie's pots. In my mind, I visualized the meals I'd had around her table and instantly felt like she was giving me a big hug. I became determined to get in the kitchen and start slinging some pots around.

Troy had a great pot selection because his grandmother stocked his kitchen, and just like my grandmothers, she believed in quality. He had nothing but the best, including a perfectly seasoned cast-iron skillet. We weren't married at the time, so this wasn't my kitchen, but it was a well-seasoned kitchen full of Troy's grandmother's love. So I felt right at home.

For a moment in time, I was able to step into a space where I felt extremely confident, giving me a respite from caring about what other people thought of me. (And even worse, what I thought about myself.) It was like the world around me stopped, and I found myself in heaven. I was an eighteen-year-old in love with the man of my dreams. A dream I had never imagined, but the feelings were so intense that I knew he had to be the one. I didn't grow up dreaming. I was busy surviving and navigating my life choices. But somehow I knew that I had chosen right this time. It brings me tears of joy thinking about it. I crossed a bridge to a better life, and I had plenty of beautiful moments growing up that instilled in me the tools I needed to care for Troy. I was equipped to nourish him back to health so that he could continue to do what he loved: playing professional football.

Feel the Fear, Cross the Bridge

It felt strange to know in my heart that I was making the right decision and still have to wrestle with all this inner doubt. I made many questionable choices throughout my eighteen years of living, and to have such clarity that this was a good one was surreal. It almost was too good to be true. As I shopped and prepped, cooked and cleaned, I reminded myself that I was writing my own story now. I had the honor of working from the lessons I had learned from the seasoned women who raised me. The pen was now in my hand. I was the author, the narrator, and the main character. Everything that I'd experienced up to this point had made me, and I was going to take that wisdom forward into a brighter future.

Crossing the bridge to a better life was not in my plan. I didn't know that bridges existed. Life in my hometown of Trenton, New Jersey, was all I knew. I wasn't looking for a new road to travel. Troy came along and built a road just for me. It was a street paved with gold, so I couldn't miss it. His misfortune that football season was a blessing in disguise.

What a gift! Being able to identify the treasure in my past amid the rubble. Because I had a bridge to cross back over, I still had access to the best parts of my story and could learn from the worst ones. I was able to bring something I was immensely proud of into a difficult time in Troy's life to reciprocate the love, care, and affirmation he graciously had given to me. I had the opportunity to contribute some of the best parts of myself through the gift of cooking and legacy-inspired recipes that had been passed down from generation to generation thanks to the seasoned women in my life. It was an honor to be able to support him in this way.

Whenever you find yourself standing at one end of a bridge—a bridge in your life that might lead to better things—you can't truly know what's on the other side. Crossing that bridge is an act of pure faith. It's far easier to stay put. To let your fear of the unknown become so consuming that it paralyzes you, keeps you from taking steps forward. But when your heart tells you that bridge leads to something better, you've got to push past the fear and use it to motivate yourself.

There's nothing wrong with being afraid. Feel the fear, but don't let it stop you from moving forward. If you believe that you're headed in the right direction, don't let your fear keep you from crossing that bridge to a better life.

Food for the Soul, One Dish at a Time

In the early 1990s, the book *Chicken Soup for the Soul* came out. It's described as a collection of inspirational true stories about ordinary people's lives. The stories were from audience members who came to hear the motivational talks given by the authors.

I have a *Chicken Soup for the Soul* story about a woman named Edith Atlay Hendricks, a.k.a. Nana Edie. There was nothing ordinary about her. She was a one-of-a-kind, extraordinary woman. One day she got a call from her granddaughter (me) asking her to take a trip to Florida to make chicken soup.

With fear and trepidation, Edie got on a plane, asked the flight attendants for a double seat belt, and braved her way to Florida to make the best pot of chicken soup you ever tasted. She did not like to fly, so this was a big deal! In order for Nana Edie to get to Florida, other ingredients needed to be added to the pot. There was a quart of courage, a cup of thoughtfulness, a heaping teaspoon of love, and a pinch of spice.

What Nana Edie didn't know was that I, too, was afraid. I was a young bride and mother figuring out my new life in a new place. Her courage was an inspiration for me, giving me the strength I needed to use the other ingredients to achieve a recipe for success. Yes, I was afraid, but I was also excited, hopeful, curious, and eager to build a new life with my husband and daughter.

Sometimes it's easy to focus on negative emotions because they can be overwhelming, consuming our thoughts and driving our decisions. I've found that bringing the positive emotions into focus helps to minimize the negative ones. I can imagine that Nana Edie's love for me minimized her fear of flying. I'm so grateful that love is more powerful than fear. When I think about the woman I am today, I know that Nana Edie is a key ingredient in my life. There would be no Tommi Vincent without Edith Atlay Hendricks.

Per Nana Edie, the key ingredient in the world's best chicken soup is a slow-roasted, well-seasoned whole chicken. After all, what's chicken soup without chicken? Every time I make my lemon herb roasted chicken, I think about my Nana Edie's chicken soup and taste the love in every bite.

Skillet Roasted Lemon *and* Rosemary Chicken *with* Potatoes

INGREDIENTS:

4- to 4½ -pound whole chicken, spatchcocked—backbone removed and butterflied

olive oil

1 tablespoon kosher salt

1 teaspoon granulated garlic

1 teaspoon onion powder

½ teaspoon black pepper

2 lemons, halved

5 rosemary sprigs

Potatoes

1½ pounds baby gold potatoes, halved

6 tablespoons butter, melted

1 teaspoon salt

¼ teaspoon black pepper

INSTRUCTIONS:

Preheat the oven to 375°F.

Put the potatoes, melted butter, salt, and pepper in a bowl and toss together. Place the potatoes in an oven-safe round skillet in a single layer.

In a bowl, combine all the chicken seasonings.

Pat the chicken dry with paper towels. Season the underside of the chicken. Place the chicken in the skillet breast side up. Brush the skin with olive oil. Season the top of the chicken.

Cut the lemons in half and squeeze the lemon juice over the chicken. Place the lemons around the chicken. Place one sprig of rosemary in the middle of the chicken and the remaining four around the chicken.

Put the chicken on the middle rack of the oven. Roast for 60 to 65 minutes, until the internal temperature is 160°F.

Cover the chicken for 10 to 15 minutes to allow it to rest. Serve hot with the potatoes and juices from the pan.

Chapter Six

Superwoman

> A woman with a voice is by definition a strong woman. But the search to find that voice can be remarkably difficult.
>
> —*Melinda Gates*

I'm the woman I am today largely because of the women who raised me. My mom, grandmothers, and aunts all contributed to the recipe of my success, with the greatest influence being my mom. When I think of resilience, she immediately comes to mind. During tough times growing up, I might have felt sad in the moment, but I somehow always believed that things would work out. That was my mom's influence. I had seen her bounce back from so many situations and had experienced her support through my own setbacks. She proved again and again that she was a survivor. I had every reason to believe that everything would be OK, because my mom would make sure of it.

At one point in my childhood, things were financially challenging for my family. There was not much room for what we wanted. If it wasn't a necessity, my siblings and I knew not to ask. This one day, after completing our Saturday morning chores, we wanted pizza. My mom had ten dollars to her name. She took her last dollars to put us first. Many times she placed us before herself.

One crisp fall Saturday, some friends and I were watching a high school football game. This was a common community gathering where I grew up. Everyone came together to cheer on their team. After the game ended, the spectators from the sold-out game made their way to the front of the school. Everyone was laughing and celebrating the victory. Well, not everyone. A girl who had a beef with my friend was plotting her vindication from a previous conflict. We saw her rapidly approaching. Suddenly, an altercation sprang up between my friend and the girl that led to multiple disputes. I don't even remember what they were upset about. All I know is that my first instinct was to call my mom. There were no cell phones back then, so I had to find a pay phone to call her collect. Once my mom accepted the collect call, I told her there was a fight.

In one swooping breath, my mom frantically yelled, "What do you mean? Where are you at? I'm on my way!"

On screeching tires, my mom zoomed into the school parking lot at the wheel of our family's candy-apple-red Pontiac Fiero two-seater sports car. Even though our home was about twenty minutes away, it seemed like she flew there in two minutes. She leaped out of the car like Superwoman, a fluorescent yellow scarf marked with black zebra stripes on her head. At this point the fight was over, but my mom's readiness to protect us at that moment was apparent.

That was my mom. I always knew I could count on her. She showed up for me time and again and taught me how to be supportive, loyal, and reliable.

I was fortunate because I could always count on not only my mom but also all the women in my family. All hell could be breaking loose in their lives, but they would suck it up to help me figure out what was going on in mine or to make it all better. Tucking away your problems, heartache, pain, and disappointments to tend to everyone else was the standard for the women in my family. I believe they learned this philosophy from their mothers, their mothers learned from their mothers, and so on. Quite naturally, I also learned this lesson and mastered it myself.

Putting Myself Aside

Not long after I arrived in Florida to support Troy through his knee injury, we traveled together to Tallahassee, where he was scheduled for surgery to repair the injury. This was a very new experience for me. I was anxious and overflowing with many questions, but I had no one to ask. But even if there had been someone to answer, I'm not sure I would have spoken up. It was important to me that Troy felt confident in my ability to show up for him. Back then, I thought that asking questions would expose my inadequacy as his partner.

Struggling with self-worth had become an unwelcome theme in my life. No matter how hard I tried to show confidence, feelings of unworthiness would always percolate to the surface! Every time those feelings reared their head, my voice was silenced. Eventually, I realized that transforming into Superwoman was helpful. I followed in the footsteps of my mom, nanas, and aunts and tucked away my own struggles to help Troy. The more I could focus on caring for him, the less I had to sit with the painful thoughts I had about myself.

Looking back on all the times my mom showed up as

Superwoman for me, I wonder what she was experiencing in her own life. I think of all the treasured memories in my Nana Edie's kitchen and wonder what she was tucking away to ensure that we left with full hearts and bellies. All I can do is wonder. The women in my family did not talk about what they were experiencing. There was no voice to narrate their story. I can relate. Finding the words to describe your own life can be difficult when you're busy tuning into the lives of those around you. In my case, it was easier to be a superwoman for my family than it was to face the voice within.

At the time, this didn't feel like losing myself or my identity. It felt perfectly normal and natural. Diving into life with Troy felt so easy. I loved him. I wanted to take care of him. Caring for other people came naturally to me, and I was good at it. My very first aspiration as a little girl was to be a wife and mother. My favorite game to play with my dolls was family. It didn't matter if it was all baby dolls, Barbies, or stuffed animals; someone was the daddy, someone was the mommy, and the rest were the children. I was still playing with my doll babies when I got pregnant at twelve years old.

Seven years later, when I was nineteen, I married Troy. My ear tuned into the voices of my husband and children, and I prioritized their needs. My voice went on inside of me, but I ignored it. I pushed aside my pain to tend to the people around me. Just like that, I was carrying forward the lesson I'd learned from the women who raised me.

A Change for Everyone

For the most part, my family understood how important these changes were to me, but I did get some pushback. My husband

and my kids had become very accustomed to the woman I was. And so the transition of releasing that selfless, caretaking behavior and showing up differently caused some angst. At first they weren't sure what was happening or how to adjust to the change.

During this time, we started a tradition where we'd meet at the table for a special family dinner where everyone would write down their dreams and then share them aloud. (We still do this today.) At the inaugural dinner, I spoke about the importance of my healing, learning to care for myself, putting myself first, and pursuing new goals that would take me outside my comfort zone. Essentially, resigning my role as Superwoman.

One of my sons spoke up and said, "Well, what about us?"

I understood his reaction, but I was also troubled by it.

I said to him, "When have I ever, in your life, not considered you? When have I ever, in our life together, not considered everyone? That will not change. What I'm saying is that the equation is incomplete if I'm not included as well."

Getting everybody on board to recognize that a better me was better for them as well took a little time and adjustment. I'd been raising this family with Troy for all of my adult life, and this change within me was also a change for them. But I did quickly show them that it was a win-win situation—that I could be a wife, a mother, and a loving and active participant in our family *without* draining myself dry. Some years later, my son told me how proud he was of me for pursuing my dreams. I knew at that moment that he got it. That made me proud. Not only was I modeling healthier behavior for my daughters, but my sons, Troy Jr., Taron, and Tanner, were also learning how to care for themselves.

Breaking the Cycle

It wasn't until much later that I realized I was part of a cycle. That I had learned to be Superwoman from the example set by the women who raised me, and because of that, I might pass that behavior along to my own daughters. I realized that my role models were doing what they had to do to survive the circumstances of their lives. As an impressionable young girl who had great admiration for them, I mimicked their behavior. There were many years while I was raising Desiré when I demonstrated the very things that the women in my life had taught me. Just moving through life, brushing aside self-care for the sake of getting things done, ignoring my own needs so that I could serve others. I was modeling that for her. I was saying to her, and later to her sister, Hadassah, "This is how you show up as a woman."

I did this unintentionally. Without realizing how harmful that selflessness could be.

Desiré was just twelve years younger than I was, so in a way we were adults moving through life together. But I also knew that I had an influence on her simply because I was her mother. I saw her begin to move through her friendships in very much the same way. She became the friend everybody called when there was a crisis. She gave all of herself to her relationships without expecting any support in return. Desiré was putting on the Superwoman cape and stepping into that role, just like I had.

It wasn't until I got into therapy and began my own healing process that I started to change my behavior and then show my daughters how to change theirs. I had to do that work before I could put down the cape. I wanted so much more for my girls than what I had learned from the women in my life. But I didn't do that work specifically so that I could help my girls unlearn the role of Superwoman. I had to save myself first, then present them with a new example of taking care of yourself.

I wanted to change the pattern of behavior that compromised my quality of life because I didn't want to suffer in silence and miss out on living a full life. But also because I needed my girls, Desiré and Hadassah, to see me fighting for myself so that they would have the courage to fight for themselves. It was important for them to see that we each hold the power to shift the narrative of our story through our deliberate choices. I knew that my choice to shift from the past to the possibilities of what could be would empower the women in my family for generations to come. My daughters, their daughters, their daughters' daughters. And that was going to start with me.

In some ways, I wish I had broken the cycle earlier. If I'd had any idea how unhealthy it was to tuck my own identity away so that I could swoop in and help the people around me, maybe I could have avoided teaching that pattern to my girls. But I cannot change the past. Honestly, the past has informed my present and paved a way for a better future for my girls and for me. So shoulda, coulda, woulda serves no purpose and would only compound the guilt and shame. I resist that type of firsthand abuse at all costs. I will not beat myself up. And neither should you. Our focus should be on what we can change right now. It took longer than I would have liked, but I made my way to get the help I needed in therapy. And I'm grateful to have had the realizations, done the work, and broken the cycle at all. It's never too early or too late to start choosing to prioritize your well-being.

You can learn to care for yourself at any age and at any stage of life. And whenever you do, you will flourish because of it.

Food for the Soul, One Dish at a Time

Before you can have any vegetables to harvest and cook, you must first plant their seeds. While they're buried in the dirt, water and sun and warmth all work to help those seeds pop open so that eventually the vegetables can reach their full potential. That incredibly complicated process first begins within the tiny seeds buried in the dirt. Big work can happen in small packages, and it all begins from the inside.

I wish I had known earlier that in order to find my voice, I would have to let the process on the inside begin. Instead of turning down the volume of my voice, I could have used it. I could have used my voice to ask all those questions that I kept secret and to use the answers to help me find the nourishment I needed to feel worthy. I could have identified the sustenance I required to become sturdy and rooted in the beauty of how I was created.

If I had to pick a vegetable that represents me, it would be collard greens. When they're in their early stages of growth, they're tender and fragile. However, as they mature, they become sturdier. Although the leaf becomes a bit tougher the longer it grows, the taste is not affected. With thoughtful and intentional cooking preparation, you can make the collard green tender again. Like this versatile plant, I'm sturdy and tender at the same time.

Collard greens are my favorite vegetable. Growing up, they adorned my family's table at every holiday. I've continued that tradition at our family celebrations. My aunt's pots of greens were so tender, they melted in your mouth. The pot liquor—the juice created from the greens steeping in the seasoning and smoked meat—was always full of rich flavor. My legacy-inspired recipe was created with her pot of greens in mind.

Collard Greens

INGREDIENTS:

6 large bunches or two 32-ounce bags of collard greens

2 pieces smoked turkey parts (optional)

1 teaspoon crushed red pepper

2 quarts chicken broth

1 tablespoon chicken or vegetable flavor
Better Than Bouillon

¼ cup sugar

2 to 3 tablespoons white distilled vinegar

2 to 3 tablespoons baking soda

Black pepper to taste

Salt to taste

INSTRUCTIONS:

Remove the stems from the greens. Stack the green leaves, roll longways, and cut into thin ribbons.

Soak the greens in water with a couple of tablespoons of baking soda. Rinse thoroughly and strain the greens. Set aside.

In a large stockpot, add chicken broth, smoked turkey (cut the surface of the meat to help the flavor release quicker), Better Than Bouillon, and crushed red pepper. Allow flavors to meld together over medium-high heat for 15 minutes.

Remove smoked turkey and set aside. Start adding greens in batches. With every batch, add a sprinkle of sugar and a dash of black pepper. Once the batch cooks down, add a new batch and repeat until all the greens are in the pot. If your pot is large enough, add everything at once.

Add all the vinegar, and salt to taste. Place the smoked turkey on top and cook until the greens are tender.

Remove the smoked turkey before serving.

Chapter Seven

The Weight Is Over

> There is a very important difference between the burdens that life puts on us and the burdens we put on our own lives: We cannot get rid of the former, but we can get rid of the latter!
>
> —Mehmet Murat ildan

All of those years playing house with my doll babies, I never imagined having five real-life doll babies of my own: Desiré, Troy Jr., Taron, Hadassah, and Tanner. The realness of it makes my heart explode with deep gratitude and an immense amount of joy.

I knew I wanted to have a family, but I didn't ever put a number to how many children I would birth. And as it turned out, each pregnancy coincided with a notable moment in my life.

In addition to being twelve years old when I gave birth to Desiré, I was heading into junior high school. Two huge life changes rolled into one.

I gave birth to Troy Jr. while I was in cosmetology school, we were moving into our newly built custom home, and Troy was at the start of his second season with the Miami Dolphins. One day I was jumping for joy at Troy getting an interception in his game. The next I was in labor and delivery, giving birth to our first son!

With Taron, I gave birth three months after opening my salon. During my pregnancy with him, I was busy coordinating the renovation of the space, which used to be the old Rocco's Pizza Place I had frequented when visiting Nana Claudia as a young girl.

Pulling up the rear, I gave birth to the twins, Hadassah and Tanner, while Troy was living in Buffalo, New York, playing for the Buffalo Bills and three months before I took a position as a cosmetology teacher at the local community college. As you can see, I stayed busy!

Words of Power

Even before all of my children had arrived, I knew myself to be a hard worker and deeply loyal. So I took to heart the question posed to me in 1994, early on in my marriage, by one of Troy's friends:

"So what are you going to do all day while Troy is at work?"

His condemning tone caused that question to replay on the loudspeaker in my mind any time I thought I wasn't doing enough. No matter how hard I worked, I always thought I could be doing more. Contentment was not easy for me to come by. I felt I needed to prove wrong all those who thought I was not the right one for Troy. And questions like that just added to my inner turmoil.

Troy's friend made a word deposit in me that I cashed in and paid the price for over many years. It amazes me how words that are spoken only once can be heard again and again over the course of a lifetime.

Words can transform your life. They carry a weight that can influence the trajectory of your future. Light words illuminate your pathway, helping give you direction toward a brighter future. They're filled with encouragement, hope, and confidence in the possibilities of who you can become. Just as I've experienced the destruction that judgmental words can cause, I've experienced the incredible power of light, loving words.

After I had Desiré, my high school teacher, Ms. Austin, changed the course of my life with her words. She was tough, but fair and would give me this look when she knew I was up to no good. It was the kind of look a mom gives to her children when they're misrepresenting who she knows them to be. A look that is full of disappointment, anger, grief, compassion, and hope all at the same time. One day, some friends and I walked into Ms. Austin's classroom as high as kites. We had smoked marijuana before coming to her class.

She called me into the hallway, looked me square in the eyes, and said, "You're better than the choices you're making."

I believed her.

Somewhere deep inside, I knew it was true and that she was right. As I took my seat at my desk, my friends asked what she'd said. A great sense of conviction came over me, and I shook my head while mumbling, "Nothing." But that was the last time I showed up to Ms. Austin's class high.

I remember another day just as clearly. When I was pregnant with Troy Jr., I was holding court and cussing like a sailor in my cosmetology class. My classmate Dawn said, "You're too intelligent to have such a limited vocabulary."

I believed her.

In the moment, however, pride would not allow me to receive

her words kindly. I told her she wasn't my mom and kept on cussing. My forty-minute drive home from school that day was a different story. I considered Dawn's words carefully. I knew she was right and decided to mind my word choices. I apologized to her in the following class.

When I gave birth to Taron, I had Troy Jr. stay the night with me. Yeah, I don't know what I was thinking! He was all over the place. If there was a wall, he was bouncing off it. I started yelling at him loudly enough to be heard at the nurses' station. A sweet nurse came in and said, "Baby, you're a loving mommy. Don't use your words to hurt him; use them to love him."

I believed her.

Immediately, I changed my tone and words, affirming that Troy Jr. was becoming a new big brother and would no longer be the baby. I invited him in closer to embrace his new baby brother. Giving birth to the twins was a new experience for me. Two babies coming out of me over the course of one bout of labor was overwhelming. Hadassah was first. She flew out at four pounds twelve ounces. Tanner, on the other hand, made a slow and grand entrance with what seemed like the entire hospital team of doctors and nurses in the room. He was breeched with the cord wrapped around his body. I was too far into labor, so a cesarean birth was not an option.

My obstetrician, Dr. Tashjin said, "Babe, you're going to have to push this baby out. You can do this. Let's go!"

I believed her.

"You're better than the choices you're making."

"You're too intelligent to have such a limited vocabulary."

"Baby, you're a loving mommy."

"You can do this. Let's go!"

The weight of these statements helped me to see a way forward. Life had become my classroom, and the instructors who showed up were my teachers, classmates, nurses, and doctors.

Words That Drag You Down

Heavy words have the opposite effect. They contain a gravity that pulls you into a dark place, making it difficult to move beyond them. These words are filled with despair, fear, hurt, and condemnation.

I experienced heavy words many times throughout my childhood. I had a friend with whom I went to elementary and junior high school. Her mother knew me and frequently invited me over for playdates when we were in elementary school. Once I entered middle school, and after giving birth to Desiré, her mother no longer treated me with the loving-kindness she once had given little Tommi.

I remember one day after middle school, my friend and I were standing outside the school building, laughing and having a good time. She and I had the same gregarious laugh—a big, wide laugh where you could see all our teeth and tonsils. And boy did we make some wonderful memories full of those out-loud laughing moments. But on this particular day, when her mom arrived to pick her up, she rolled down the car window and told my friend, "I don't want you being Tommi's friend anymore," as if I wasn't standing there.

My friend never made eye contact with me. She grabbed her book bag, got in the car, and drove away.

On my walk home, I chewed on those words repeatedly until they became fully digested in my system. Moving forward, I assumed that all of my friends' moms had the same sentiments.

This daunting thought led me to believe that I no longer belonged with my peers.

When Troy Jr. was three months old, I pursued my first job as a stylist at a salon just minutes away from my home. The owner asked me to come in to do a color and blow-dry as part of the interviewing process. In cosmetology school, I won multiple awards and became one of the students whom clients would request by name at the school's salon. No doubt I was nervous, with sweaty palms and butterflies in my stomach. But I was confident that I could execute on the expectations of the demo portion of the interview. I had many repetitions of these types of services under my belt from the school salon.

I dropped Troy Jr. off at day care and hustled my way to the salon for my big day. The client who was scheduled as my salon audition had two inches of fully gray roots with jet-black ends. Her hair texture was very fine. I welcomed her to my chair and proceeded to prep her for the color application. I went to the color room, picked out the color, and mixed in the developer. A few of the employees were back there cheering me on. It was very encouraging.

I proceeded with the color application, then I styled her hair. She was pleased with the results, and I was relieved to be finished. The employees who were encouraging me in the back added their compliments to the results. All but one woman, who never even said hello.

After I was done, the owner instructed me to sit in the reception area. I waited anxiously for what seemed like forever.

Finally, she sat down next to me and said, "You're not a good fit for our salon."

Words continued to come out of her mouth, but I didn't hear

them. I got stuck on the rejection. The back of my eyes filled with tears. I fought with everything I had to keep them from falling, but the tears won that day. As she talked, I cried. It was an ugly cry too. The last thing I heard her say was, "The manager wants to pass on hiring you."

As you might have guessed, the manager was the woman who did not say hello. Nor did she say goodbye. The pain of rejection that flooded my soul consumed me in a way I cannot explain. Maybe I really wasn't a good fit for this salon. None of that mattered to me. The rejection had taken over.

I pulled myself together and shamefully walked out of the salon. So different from how I'd walked in. The drive to pick up Troy Jr. from day care was somber and silent. Not only did I have to contend with the rejection, but also, as I processed more, I realized that I had to go home and tell Troy I didn't get the job. There was a shift from rejection to embarrassment to unworthiness. Troy had demonstrated only love and support for me, but somehow I believed his takeaway would still be that I wasn't good enough.

In a matter of minutes, I conjured up the worst possible outcome. Troy would think all those people who said I wasn't the right one were correct. Before I knew it, I had arrived at Troy Jr.'s school. All of what I was feeling was still rattling around inside me, but I knew it couldn't come in with me to greet my precious baby boy. I swallowed it all up, including the narrative I was telling myself, and put on a brave face for my son.

I did end up securing a position at a different salon, but the rejection of this moment—coupled with the fear of a similar outcome—came with me to every interview. That painful experience led me to question my value.

The Cost of Unkindness

Not long after giving birth to the twins, I had a family funeral to attend. Although funerals bring great sadness, there's also an element of joy in reuniting with family you haven't seen in a long time. As Troy and I exited the church, I noticed one of my relatives whom I hadn't seen in years. Full of happiness and excitement, we leaned in to embrace each other.

He pulled back and said, "Wow, girl, you got fat!"

An awkward smile spread across my face as the corners of my lips quivered. Eventually, others surrounded us, and as the crowd distracted him, my insecurity enveloped me. This insecurity harnessed my bright smile and warmness that were endearing qualities familiar to my family. I could feel myself shrinking in my "fat" body.

With nowhere to go, I did my best in the moment to enjoy reconnecting with my family. As soon as I thought I had spent the appropriate amount of time visiting with everyone, I left. But that moment stayed with me. I was actively working out to get back into shape after having the twins, and I was feeling good about my progress. But after that comment, the grace I had been giving myself was gone. I painstakingly looked at myself in the mirror and judged myself harshly when I saw that my clothes did not fit.

"I don't want you being Tommi's friend anymore."

"You're not a good fit for our salon."

"Wow, girl, you got fat!"

It doesn't take much for words to chip away at the soul or to weigh us down. They affix to the heart and create a heaviness. Heavy with self-doubt, lack of self-worth, and self-loathing. A statement doesn't have to be said with malicious intent to create negative consequences. A few words spoken to me in brief moments had long-term effects. I wasn't equipped to let these weights go on my own. I accumulated more and more, year over year. My heart got heavier and heavier. Until one day I was so weighted down that I couldn't get up from my king-size mattress.

Food for the Soul, One Dish at a Time

On some special occasions like the winter holidays, birthdays, and monumental celebrations, I pull out all the stops when I'm cooking. I use my best pots, fine china, and legacy-inspired recipes with an extensive list of ingredients. As I matured in life, I realized that I hadn't been going all out and using my best dishes and recipes, and I wondered what I was waiting for to create the moments that make the memories. Holidays and birthdays are annual occasions. Monumental occasions are not as frequent. What if next year doesn't come, or I'm not here to celebrate the next significant moment? It took many years for me to realize that *I myself* was a special occasion.

In fact, we're all special enough to celebrate daily. None of us should wait to enjoy life.

Just think about those occasions when you gathered with loved ones and all the fond memories that were made. I have a treasure chest full of memories, family members enjoying one another's company while chowing down on all the food that was prepared with love, listening to the soundtrack of laughter, and the friendly bickering happening in the next room during the spades tournament. I want to create as many of those memories as possible so that, for generations to come, my children's children will have beautiful remember-when stories.

There are a few staple dishes that always accompany these memories. One of them is baked macaroni and cheese.

Baked Macaroni *and* Cheese

INGREDIENTS:

2 lbs. elbow macaroni, cooked al dente

3 tablespoons butter—for roux

3 tablespoons flour—for roux

1 quart half-and-half

2 cups Colby-Jack cheese, shredded

7 cups sharp cheddar cheese, shredded

1 cup Gruyère cheese, shredded

8 ounces cream cheese, cubed

4 eggs

1½ teaspoons salt

1 teaspoon pepper

Paprika for garnish

Cooking spray

3-quart rectangular casserole dish

INSTRUCTIONS:

Preheat the oven to 350°F.

In a saucepan, add butter and flour on medium-high heat. Whisk until smooth. Gradually pour in the half-and-half. Bring to a boil and reduce heat to medium.

Add Colby-Jack, cream cheese, salt, and pepper. Whisk until smooth. Remove from heat and set aside.

In a large bowl, add cooked elbow macaroni noodles, Gruyère, and 3½ cups of sharp cheddar. Combine ingredients until evenly distributed.

In a separate bowl, whisk the eggs, then pour them into the bowl with the noodles and grated cheeses. Combine until completely distributed throughout.

Add ¼ cup of the cheese sauce into the macaroni and cheese mixture and mix well. This small addition will help temper the sauce into the macaroni and cheese so that you don't end up with scrambled eggs. Slowly pour the remaining cheese sauce while mixing, until completely combined.

Pour ingredients into a casserole dish. Layer the top with the remaining sharp cheddar and sprinkle with paprika. Spray a sheet of aluminum foil with cooking spray and loosely place the sprayed side of the foil on top of the macaroni and cheese. This will keep the cheese from sticking to the top of the foil.

Bake for 20 minutes, covered.

Remove foil and bake an additional 20 to 25 minutes. Remove from the oven and let macaroni and cheese cool for 15 minutes prior to serving.

Chapter Eight

Somebody Turned On the Lights

> Give light and people will find the way.
>
> —*Ella Baker*

All around me was evidence that I had accomplished a lot in my life. I was married to a wonderful man with a celebrated career. I had a daughter who was a college graduate and who was advancing her career in New York City; a high schooler and middle schooler who were both stellar student athletes, being recruited from colleges around the nation; and twins who were the star pupils of their class. My family was healthy and thriving. Yet somehow I felt like a failure. I didn't see myself in their accomplishments. Accepting defeat, I surrendered to my bed, immobilized by my weighted blanket, filled with the negative thoughts I had about myself and the harmful words of others. I was in a dark place.

How did I get here?

It wasn't one thing. It was the accumulation of many things

unaddressed. Truthfully, I didn't know that I needed to deal with anything until my mental state got so bad that I could no longer function. Had I been able to press through my depression, it's very likely I would have just kept going, never knowing how compromised the quality of my life was.

I was in desperate need of help. My first inclination was to ask God to send me help; I needed a lifeline. Shortly after I sent up a prayer, I attended a women's conference. Little did I know that help was on the way.

As I sat in my seat, numb to everything around me, a powerful voice came through the speakers. Suddenly, I could feel my feet under my body. I awakened from my slumber. My heart started beating fast, and hope pulsed through my veins. Hastily, I flipped through the program to see who this woman was who had captivated my attention. Before I could find her name, she said, "I'm Dr. Woods, a licensed psychologist." Truthfully, I didn't know what a psychologist did, so I pulled out my phone and googled it.

As she continued in her presentation, it felt like she and I were the only ones in the room. She was speaking directly to me. I knew that God had answered my request. Dr. Woods was my lifeline. Although I was still in a dark place, I left the conference believing that Dr. Woods was my answer. Hope replaced despair, and for the first time in a long while, I was looking forward to tomorrow.

A Conflicted Mind

The next day, I reached out to the conference organizer for Dr. Woods's contact information and called her immediately. She didn't pick up, so I left a voicemail. I was nervous. I tried to choose my words carefully. I didn't want something I said in the voicemail to prevent her from working with me. Here I was, in the fight of my life, and I didn't believe I was worthy of getting help!

Throughout the day, I checked my phone to make sure I hadn't accidentally turn the ringer off. Or had walked away and missed her call. Early in the evening, the call came. My heart dropped to the pit of my stomach.

Oh no. It's her, I thought.

I felt so conflicted. I had desperately wanted her to call. Then when she did, I started freaking out. I stared at the screen for a few seconds before gathering the courage to press the button and begin the call—the call I had been waiting for all day.

"Hello, Tommi. This is Dr. Woods. I received your voicemail. How can I help you, dear?"

I didn't quite know how to respond to the question. For whatever reason, my mind was clinging to the idea that there was a right and a wrong answer. A part of me felt embarrassed that I was struggling and broken. Mostly, I felt pressure to convince her to choose me. I didn't want to screw this up!

Because I was a bundle of nerves, my voice was shaky. Slowly, the words started coming out of my mouth.

"I've been struggling to get out of bed, and I don't know why."

She fired off a few more questions. The more I spoke, the calmer I became. After we hung up, I felt a sense of relief. I had done it. As foreign as this felt to me, there was no way I could navigate this darkness alone. I needed someone to turn on a light so that I could see. And I had found the person I knew could do that for me and with me.

The Road to Healing

For two years, I traveled an hour and twenty minutes each way to my weekly therapy session with Dr. Woods. I will never forget my first drive. Tears of anguish blurred my vision as I got on the highway and set out on my journey to discover what was wrong with me. Every mile became harder and harder to drive. The closer I got to her office, the more intimidated I felt about facing one of the greatest challenges of my life.

When I was growing up, there were a few people in my life who experienced something I heard the adults call a nervous breakdown. One day they would be around, and the next they would disappear for a while. A couple of times, I went with my Nana Edie to the psychiatric hospital to pick them up. No one ever came home the same. They moved slower, and their personalities were duller. They lost their vibrancy. Any trace of the liveliness that had once filled their faces was replaced by blank stares.

I believed that help was waiting for me once I arrived at my destination, but I was also afraid. What if what I saw in those other people happened to me? I would go into Dr. Woods's office one way and come out another. Or even worse, she would send me to the psychiatric hospital. I had no idea what to expect. Because we didn't discuss mental health growing up, I assumed the outcomes all looked the same. There were no levels to mental illness. The spectrum was either normal or the psychiatric ward, with nothing in between. I didn't have these extreme assumptions with other health issues. If I got a cold, I'd go to the doctor's office, get my diagnosis, pick up my prescription, and expect to get better. I didn't leap to the conclusion that something was gravely wrong with me. I simply didn't know enough about mental health to understand that it was nuanced and complicated but also treatable. Just like a cold.

A Light in the Darkness

With no more stretches of highway in front of me, I made it into the driveway and parked my truck. Her office was in her home. I made my way up the cobblestone path to the huge wooden doors with glass panels laced with intricate iron details. It was time to get to work, but first I had to take the courageous step of ringing the doorbell. At this point, I knew there was no turning back. I reached out my pointer finger and activated my help. I could hear her footsteps approaching. It sounded like a giant was coming down the hallway. Then Dr. Woods opened the door and greeted me with a warm smile.

"Come on in, dear," she said.

Following her lead down a long hallway adorned with family photos and achievements, I took my seat in her office.

Where's the couch? I wondered.

Every movie I'd ever seen where someone was in therapy, they lay on a couch. There was no couch. There were three chairs, lots of books, and a few plants. It didn't look like what I'd imagined. Surprisingly, there was a warmth and a sense of comfort to her office. This was a very welcome surprise. It felt like home.

Dr. Woods was a seasoned woman in her early seventies. She was tall in stature, wore large eyeglass frames, and set her hair in a slicked-back bun pulled very tight. Her fingers were long and bony, which I noticed straightaway because she spoke with her hands. What sealed the deal for me was her no-nonsense personality. This was a very familiar characteristic. It reminded me a lot of myself. She was direct in her communication, which was something I appreciated.

There were fifty minutes on the clock, and not one of them was wasted. I must have talked for forty minutes of our time together. In that one session, every part of me knew that this was exactly what I needed. Dr. Woods possessed a master key that unlocked a door in my heart, out of which the issues of my life started flowing. They were no longer locked away in the darkness.

If one session could have this level of impact, I knew that continuing to work with Dr. Woods over many sessions could help me find my way out of the darkness. She had a great deal of life and family experience, and I could tell that she would use it all to support me. Along with her expertise, there was much wisdom that came out in our sessions.

On my drive home that day, the tears still flowed, but this time my vision was clearer. Yes, there was more work to be done, but I was finally beginning to see myself. Dr. Woods had turned on the light, and I started to like what I saw.

Stepping Out of the Darkness

I didn't tell anybody that I was battling with depression until after I'd had multiple sessions of therapy. Troy had no idea. He worked in New York during the week, and I was at home in Virginia with the little kids. I'd found all kinds of fun ways to keep them entertained—picnics on blankets, watching TV, playing simple games that didn't need my attention—so that I could stay in bed all day. Nearby but not really engaged. When Troy came home on the weekends, he was exhausted from working and traveling, so it was easy enough to hide my struggles. I would muster up enough strength to make us a meal, then I would say, "Let's just lie on the couch and watch TV." Then I was free to nestle back into my blanket and tune out the world.

But after I'd done some work with Dr. Woods and could tell that my life was about to change direction, I knew I couldn't keep it to myself much longer. I needed to tell Troy. I did it very casually. One morning as he was walking into the bathroom and I was walking out, I said, "Oh yeah, by the way, I've been so depressed the past few months that I couldn't get out of bed, but I'm in therapy now."

He was stunned. He couldn't believe I'd hidden all of this from him for so long. But I had mastered masking my pain. One thing I pride myself on is that anything I'm going to do, I'm going to do it well. And I did that very well. I wore that mask like a pro.

After I told him the truth, there was a period of time when it felt like Troy was handling me with kid gloves. That bothered me a little, to be treated like I was made of glass. But I understood it because therapy was not commonplace for me or for him. As I mentioned earlier, growing up, we associated mental illness with total breakdowns, straitjackets, people being carted off to hospitals. Our friends and family members didn't see therapists. Or if they did, they never talked about it. What I was going through was very foreign to Troy. I don't think he knew how to support me, and he was responding out of a desire to not see me hurting.

Honestly, though, Dr. Woods was so good, I really didn't care how my family reacted to the news that I was in therapy. I recognized that in order for me to do what I needed to do to save myself, I couldn't care anymore. I couldn't care what Troy thought. I couldn't care what the kids thought. I had to focus on myself so that I could get well. Were my family members wondering if I was crazy? That was their problem. I let them figure it out.

I had never shown up for myself like that before. But now that Dr. Woods had turned on that light, I wasn't going to let anyone turn it off again.

Food for the Soul, One Dish at a Time

Living a life riddled with trauma and difficulties can leave you with a hardened heart. My heart was hardened, and the arteries were clogged with a great deal of pain and sorrow, preventing all my love from flowing. I could be sitting in a roomful of joy and laughter, yet part of me would be unable to partake of the full experience of the moment. I restricted myself from enjoying life too much because I believed pain and suffering were the consequences of my choices.

Even if no one was causing me harm, I would punish myself because I believed I deserved it. That punishment might have looked like I was angry for no reason. I could be laughing and having a good time when suddenly a spirit of anger would take hold of me. My smile would turn upside down, and I would transport inwardly, disconnecting from everyone around me.

Troy, confused by the shift, would ask, "What's wrong?"

Annoyed by the concern, I would respond, "*Nothing*." My mood would end up shifting everyone's experience. I tried hard to shake it, but it had such a grip on me.

Dr. Woods helped me to realize that I needed to be tenderized. I was no longer in an environment where I required protecting. Although I couldn't change the past, I had the power to determine how I would respond to it. I no longer had to be tough.

So, in honor of that lesson, I'm sharing my legacy-inspired chuck roast with mushroom gravy. It's tender and will make you feel right at home, like I did in Dr. Woods's office.

Chuck Roast *with* Mushroom Gravy

INGREDIENTS:

3- to 3.5-pound chuck roast

1 tablespoon salt

1 teaspoon black pepper

16 ounces sliced white mushrooms

2 tablespoons olive oil

32 ounces vegetable stock

1 tablespoon beef Better Than Bouillon

3 tablespoons cornstarch

INSTRUCTIONS:

Preheat the oven to 375°F.

Pat beef dry with paper towels. Cut into medium-size pieces. Place in a bowl and toss in seasoning until evenly coated.

Add oil to a skillet over medium heat. Add beef and sear meat on all sides.

Add the mushrooms on top of the beef.

Add broth, Better Than Bouillon, and cornstarch to a bowl. Whisk together until well combined. Pour around the sides of the pan, not over the mushrooms.

Cover with an oven-safe lid. Bake in the oven for 3 hours.

Serve warm over rice.

Chapter Nine

Walking in the Light

> When you recover or discover something that nourishes your soul and brings joy, care enough about yourself to make room for it in your life.
>
> —Jean Shinoda Bolen

Before I had my hysterectomy, I was managing life just fine, or so I thought. Spending fifteen days a month on my menstrual cycle with debilitating cramps, zapped of energy and motivation, became the norm. I planned my life accordingly. That gave me fifteen days, plus or minus a few, to be productive each month. It wasn't until after I had the procedure done that I realized how much my quality of life had been compromised.

I had a very similar epiphany as I progressed through therapy. For many years, I was just getting by. My life was not without wonderful experiences, but the problem was that all of me was not embracing them. The parts of my identity that I believed disqualified me from being worthy of the best were left out. Teenage mom Tommi, abused Tommi, rejected Tommi, not good enough

Tommi were all denied the opportunity to enjoy this new life God had blessed me with. Those parts of my identity were tucked away, deep down inside. All the words that people weaponized against me, knowingly or not, caused me to retreat. Instead of celebrating what I had overcome—and honoring the parts of me that had endured so that I could survive—I punished them.

Working with Dr. Woods helped me reclaim those pieces of myself. Slowly, I saw how dim my life had become and how I had accepted that as my reality. And then, as I turned on more and more lights, I came back to life and back to myself. Those sessions transformed me.

So did the long commute! Driving an hour and twenty minutes each way gave me the time and space to process everything Dr. Woods and I had talked about, which made a huge difference. I made progress in every session, but it didn't always feel that way at first. Sometimes coming out of a session in which we'd covered some particularly painful subjects, I felt exhausted and empty. But once I got in my car and started driving, alone on the road in the quiet, I could replay our conversation again. That space between her door and mine gave me the opportunity to absorb what I'd said and learned.

When I walked into my home, I wasn't bringing in the weight of our conversations. I'd taken the time to understand and make peace with my progress so that when my precious babies greeted me with their smiling faces, I was ready to receive them. All because I had that commute to process.

I believe that time for reflection is so important. When you're navigating challenging terrain in your life, carving out space to process your experiences makes the journey much easier. If you're getting help from a therapist, and the people in your life are aware of the process, they may unknowingly hold back your progress. The people who love you may want to fix you themselves by offering advice or solutions. Or they may be worried and eager to make sure you're OK. If they crowd you with their good intentions before you've had a chance to process on your own, they may intercept what you've experienced in your therapy or even negate it.

Healing from past pain and trauma is something that must happen in stages. Naming what hurt you and talking it through with a therapist is a crucial first step. But I learned that reflecting on my therapy sessions was almost as important as the sessions themselves. I needed to give my learnings time to breathe and to give myself space to process them. I had to absorb them into my being before I could really get to work and make myself better.

Inner Turmoil

Every fiber of my being fought so that I could cross the bridge to a new life, and therapy showed me that I deserved to experience that life to its fullest. When I first started seeing Dr. Woods, the diminished version of me kept me from showing up to my own life in full capacity. But session after session, the light got brighter and brighter. The parts of my life that I had viewed as tragic came into view as triumphant. The beauty of who I was, including all my life experiences, came into focus.

When I started my healing journey, I didn't recognize how bad things were in my life. There's a flip side to that, which is that I also didn't know how good things could be. Before therapy, I believed I had lost the right to want anything better for my life. I really believed that, because I had my daughter at age twelve, I would always be a huge disappointment to my parents. So when I made questionable choices and had to deal with the results, in my mind, I was getting exactly what I deserved.

As I was going through therapy, I realized that wasn't the truth. I also realized that I was a pretty special woman and that what I had experienced in my life was remarkable. I overcame some incredible challenges and setbacks, but I'd never considered my life to be hard. I never considered what it must have taken for twelve-year-old Tommi to give birth to a baby and then to go through high school and weather an abusive relationship. I assumed that was normal. It never even crossed my mind that I had been brave and strong and resilient. I never allowed myself to be proud of the unbreakable woman I had become.

Therapy was the turning point. I found myself thinking, *Look at all you've endured in your life. Girl, you're remarkable.*

Beyond surviving the bad, therapy helped me to recognize the good. Despite all the darkness, I was in a loving relationship with an amazing husband. I had wonderful, brilliant children and a warm, stable home. I'm not saying it was perfect, but it was good. So good. And I had built that life against all odds.

My past was painful, and I wouldn't wish it on anyone, but it definitely played into the woman I became. It forged me and made me unshakable. My experiences added so many tremendous attributes to who I am as a person. I am a strong woman. I am resilient. I view all those things as valuable, important qualities, and I'm not looking to shed any of them. Those aspects of myself get to be present, even in my effort to love myself, take care of myself, and grow as a woman. It's all part of who I am, and I celebrate it all.

Ripple Effects

During the course of my marriage, we weathered difficult times and the growing pains of our children. Throughout it all, the dinner table was my gift to my family. Both then and now, if anyone is going through a tough situation, I'll cook up a hug for them to soothe their weary soul. It's a pulse check to make sure that everyone is OK.

This includes me. Everyone knows that if I'm not cooking, they should check in with me because I may not be doing well. I've learned that when my gift of cooking turns off, my light is dimming. I'm not referring to an occasional feeling of not wanting to cook. We all want to rest and order takeout sometimes, including me. I mean if I stop cooking for a long time, many days or weeks in a row. My family and friends know that if I'm avoiding the kitchen, it means I've started to lose my desire to do something that nourishes my soul and gives me joy.

The flip side of that can show up as resentment, though. If I'm avoiding the kitchen and not cooking as much, that affects the people around me. Fewer home-cooked meals, not as many groceries in the refrigerator and pantry. Depending on the people and the circumstances, someone may think there's some ill intent behind you avoiding the thing that you love, especially if it's beneficial for them. Instead of seeing a change in your behavior—avoiding something that you love and that defines you—as an indication that there's something amiss, they may take it personally. They may say, "You don't ever do this anymore." They may express disappointment.

It's a natural reaction and usually one that happens instinctively. The people who say these things don't mean to be hurtful. But they can cause you to go further inward, to feel attacked and retreat into yourself. When you're hurting enough to avoid your favorite activities, you're vulnerable. You're in a place where you need understanding, you need compassion, you need empathy from the people around you because you're struggling.

It can be difficult to do so, but I believe it's important for us to use our words when this occurs. To articulate what's happening and why your behaviors have changed so that your loved ones will understand. Reactions like this present an opportunity for you to explain who you are and how you're experiencing life in the moment. It's easy to get defensive and assume that they should know what's going on. But how would they know if you've never talked about it? And if your response is to retreat inward, you're just going to keep taking the blows they're dealing out. All because you haven't used your voice to articulate what's going on.

I believe that if people care about you and they love you, they'll listen and empathize without fully understanding. Even if the changes you're experiencing cause disruption in their lives. Being open and discussing your struggles gives the people who love you an opportunity to show up for you. Because when people really love you, giving them that information allows them to love you in a greater way.

When you abandon the things you love to do, you're making your way into the darkness. But it's important to recognize that as you're working through your pain and this state that you're in, the people around you are also in the darkness. Because they don't know what you're struggling to overcome. So if you're able to share, do so. Not because you want them to fix you or to provide a solution. And if they offer, be clear: That's not the point of sharing. It's to show them why you're doing what you're doing.

When you share, you say, "The point is to turn the light on for you too. Because I need you to see me."

As my self-discovery journey progressed, visions of Nana Edie cooking in her kitchen flooded my soul. It was like watching a nostalgic movie reel of a kind, warmhearted woman who found her way to healing through soul food therapy. She was feeding others as she fed herself, doing both simultaneously. How did I know this? Because I began to experience it myself. Cooking became a practice that saved my life. All the memories of Nana Edie feeding our family, our community, and all who needed nourishment crystalized. I knew that I, too, had this gift. The feeding works both ways; it heals the cook and the people seated at her dinner table.

I found that the process of cooking activated a sense of calm for my mind, body, and soul. I became fully awake. Looking back on my life through therapy, I realized that there was never a time when I wasn't cooking. During the good and the bad times, cooking became the hug I needed. It invoked the same feeling I got while spending time in my Nana Edie's kitchen. As I was working on myself, I was in the kitchen often, cooking up my healing one dishes at a time. I didn't fully realize the power and purpose of it until I started therapy.

Desiré took notice of my love for cooking and gifted me with a wooden heart spoon. She wasn't aware that I was cooking my way through my healing. This spoon became the bandage to mend my broken heart. It became a signature utensil and is now my infamous love spoon. It became my weapon of warfare. I was slaying depression one stir at a time, simultaneously putting all of my love, strength, and courage into every dish I made. This was a legacy-inspired recipe for healing that I looked forward to passing along to my daughters. Everyone who has been part of my journey knows that when the love spoon comes out, it's about to go down. The food that is prepared nourishes deep down in the soul; it feels like comfort and tastes like home.

The Sacred Kitchen

I never considered my ability to cook as an anointing, a special gift from God. I come from a legacy of outstanding cooks, and for me it was just something we did with ease. But as I reflected on occasions throughout my childhood and as a woman with a family of my own, I recognized that our time around the table was much more than filling our bellies. I realized that there was this presence of love that melted our cares away and caressed our souls. My anointing to serve love on a plate is a blessing that has been passed down from generation to generation. In my family, cooking is the gift that keeps on giving.

There are many occasions that have brought my family to the table to break bread, including celebrating our love and support for one another. A key takeaway from my therapy sessions was the importance of savoring those good times. I call them gratitude moments. They allow us to put the world on pause. Providing an opportunity to set aside the weights that make life heavy and to exchange them for light moments that make us feel free. In these instances, we get to capture memories we wouldn't trade for anything in the world. As we eat, talk, and laugh, life doesn't feel hard. It feels just right.

The Solitary Table

Equally as important, I have learned to offer the healing power of the table to myself. That looks like me taking the time to nourish my soul. Preparing a meal for one. Sitting down with no distractions and giving myself undivided attention. The menu consists of food that makes my heart smile while my feet do a little dance. Adding a journal and pen to my place setting to write down new ideas and notable thoughts. My preference is to sit outside and listen to my favorite soundtrack: nature.

The first time I created this setting for myself, I paused, took a deep breath, and smiled. It was a welcome departure from eating at the counter while doing five hundred other things in between bites. Every time I ate that way, by the time I got around to finishing my food, it was cold and unenjoyable. I was eating out of necessity instead of for nourishment. Slowing down the pace of life and embracing time at the table taught me how to conduct my own pulse check. I hate that it took my world going dark to recognize that I was in trouble. But I'm glad I acquired enough self-awareness to see that I was deserving of the same care and nourishment that I extended to others.

A New Way, a Bigger Table

Just getting by was no way to live. My heart breaks a bit for the women who raised me. Knowing that they, too, lived in this way, missing out on the best that life had to offer. I honestly believe that the fire that burns inside me to pursue healing is intensified because I'm fighting for them as well. Therapy wasn't a tool they were given. But I was given it as a lifeline. For that, I'm grateful. I will continue to use the embers I received from those special women to fuel my fire, and I will think of them every time my light gets brighter.

Given what I came to understand as I progressed through therapy, I knew I wasn't the only woman in my circle experiencing this. The stories of heartache and pain from the women I came to know and love throughout my womanhood were numerous. The tears were enough to create rivers in the sand. My experience empowered me to choose a better way to live, and I had acquired some ingredients for success. It was time for me to create a longer table, add more chairs, and invite women to receive a big old Nana Edie hug.

Food for the Soul, One Dish at a Time

My healing journey wasn't easy. I worked hard to overcome all that life had dished up. Yet there was a tenderness throughout the process. Every step of the way, my life got sweeter and sweeter. I learned to not focus on what was wrong. I chose to home in on all that was right. My life consistently improved as I maintained the work required to overcome.

Life's journey is not a destination. It goes on until there is no more life to live. Until that day comes, I'm committed to working on my mental health to become a better version of myself so that I can live my best life. I anticipate that my life will become sweeter as the days go by, even with some bitterness along the way.

In honor of sweet days ahead, I'm sharing my legacy-inspired sweet potato pie recipe. I knew the day would come when it would be my turn to make a coveted family dessert staple. I knew just who to ask—my aunt Dolline. The filling of her sweet potato pie is so luscious. The secret ingredient is heavy cream. I got to put the recipe to the test when I made Thanksgiving dinner for Troy and several of his Philadelphia Eagles teammates and their families.

I could make homemade pie crust, but why, when there are great-tasting premade frozen ones? Some grocery stores make fresh pie shells during the holidays, and you can find them in the prepared food section. It reminds me that, in life, we don't have to start everything from scratch. We can benefit from the experience of others who have tested and developed recipes for success.

Sweet Potato Pie

INGREDIENTS:

2 8-inch pie crusts, frozen (My favorite brands are Oronoque Orchards or Marie Callender's.)

Pie filling

3 pounds of sweet potatoes, baked

1 cup brown sugar

½ cup granulated sugar

8 tablespoons butter, softened

1 teaspoon cinnamon

⅛ teaspoon nutmeg

Pinch of salt

1 teaspoon vanilla extract

½ cup heavy cream

3 large eggs

INSTRUCTIONS:

Preheat the oven to 350°F.

Bake sweet potatoes until soft and a fork pierces through the center of the potatoes easily, approximately 1 hour.

While potatoes are still warm, peel them.

Using a stand or hand mixer, add sweet potatoes to the mixing bowl. Using the paddle attachment, mix until smooth. Take off the paddle and rinse off the stringy pieces coiled around the attachment. Place the paddle back on the mixer and add in the softened butter. Keep the mixer on medium-low and add the spices and vanilla. Once the butter is completely dissolved into the sweet potatoes, add the heavy cream until thoroughly blended. Add in one egg at a time, until all the eggs are completely mixed in.

Pour the batter evenly between the pie shells. Bake for 55 to 60 minutes, until the filling puffs up and the center is supple but not jiggly.

Allow the pies to cool before serving to give them time to set.

Chapter Ten

Breaking Bread and Mending Hearts

Meanwhile, the moment we get tired in the waiting, God's Spirit is right alongside helping us along. If we don't know how or what to pray, it doesn't matter. He does our praying in and for us, making prayer out of our wordless sighs, our aching groans. He knows us far better than we know ourselves, knows our pregnant condition, and keeps us present before God. That's why we can be so sure that every detail in our lives of love for God is worked into something good.

—*Romans 8:26–28 (MSG)*

Imagine that there's a giant in your life, something that feels larger than life itself, and you don't even know where to begin to fight it. Then imagine finding out that you had everything you needed inside you all along to defeat the giant. This was me. I didn't know to dream for better or to expect more. You don't know what you don't know—until you do! Achieving this level of revelation cannot be kept to oneself. At least, that was my experience. It was so good, I had to share it.

After many therapy sessions, I felt confident and ready to conquer the world. One day, I was sitting in my worn-out black leather office chair, crying my eyeballs out. Each tear mirrored the sound of the rain outside my window. As the tears puddled on my desk, I could feel my broad shoulders curving in and my posture shrinking. I had just wrapped up a meeting with a guy for whom I was doing some consulting work. I had confronted him about a function I no longer wanted to be responsible for doing. He looked at me with pure evil in his eyes, curled his lip, and said, "You don't have a choice." Yes, his tone bothered me, but it was the familiar look in his eyes that rocked me to my core. I had seen that look many times in my abusive relationship. All those old emotions welled up in me. I swallowed them down, keeping them in check until I was no longer in his presence. But as soon as I was alone, those emotions erupted out of me like a volcano.

I shouted at the top of my lungs while pounding my fist on the desk, "God, I hate this!" I was furious with myself. I didn't understand why I hadn't spoken up for myself. There I was, feeling like I'd lost my voice again. It was like he'd sucked the soul out of my body, and my mouth was sealed shut.

I sobbed for every bit of ten minutes, when suddenly, this vision flashed before my eyes. I saw myself speaking with women in large numbers. It was so real. I felt like I was in the room with them. I called out to God again, "What are you talking about? No one even knows my name!"

A surreal peace washed over me. The tears stopped. I heard

a still, small voice say, "The one who is working on your behalf knows who you are." The voice wasn't audible, but I heard it very clearly in my spirit. The tears started back up, but this time it felt different. It was an overwhelming sense of gratitude.

Making the Right Changes

Circling back to the moment when I trashed myself for not speaking up to the man who'd been so disrespectful to me, it didn't take long to realize that I had stood up for myself, loud and clear, through the actions that followed our conversation. Without hesitation, I walked away from that consulting position and reported him to his boss. My willingness to sever ties with the relationship and to not rationalize his behavior was a major breakthrough. It was evidence of the progress I had made as a result of the therapy. At first, I got stuck on the moment at the desk and claimed defeat. I had predetermined what standing up for myself looked like. But soon afterward, I recognized the victory of exercising my right to walk away from an unhealthy working relationship. Young Tommi could not have been more proud!

Months passed, and I held tightly to the God moment I'd had in my office. It was as if a baby started growing inside me. Visions of gathering with women started flooding my mind. Each thought grew more and more, just like a baby grows month by month, until a full picture emerged. Before my eyes was a fully formed plan for women's retreats. A space where the women in my circle could take a seat at my table to receive much-needed nourishment.

And my family had the perfect location, affectionately known as the cabin. Troy and I had built a home on Lake Gaston in the early 2000s. Before the cabin was fully constructed, my friend

Latrina and I stood on the wood plank floors looking out over the lake and prayed. In that moment, I heard a still small voice that said, "This will be a place of restoration." At the time, a women's retreat was not on my mind, nor had I begun my battle with depression. I was very green in my approach to life and excited about what that restoration would look like for my family. Little did I know that I was the one who would need restoring.

Fast-forward to 2014, and the cabin would become the place of restoration for my first women's retreat. As the vision came into greater focus, I started scribbling out notes and drawing diagrams. Not sharing the details with anyone, I quietly started planning. I wasn't sure if I asked my friends to join me for a retreat that they would want to attend. That sounded too much like self-love, which was a foreign concept at the time. I had the perfect plan. In the summer of 2014, I would be celebrating my fortieth birthday. It was a significant milestone, and I knew I could get them to celebrate with me. The twist was that they'd be the guests of honor, and I would be celebrating them. I wanted them to experience a space that put them front and center to introduce them to my concept of firsthand love.

Growing up as the baby in the rank and file of my siblings, the vast majority of my clothing was hand-me-downs. Although they'd been worn before, they were new to me. I remember being excited to receive them, especially outfits I'd admired seeing my older sisters wear. It wasn't until I got older, started working, and bought brand-new clothes for myself that I valued having the firsthand experience of receiving my own. Firsthand love is a lot like that. We're in a position to love ourselves. Once we put in the work to understand what we like and need, we can put ourselves in a position to love ourselves through deliberate actions.

Although receiving love from others is important, experiencing firsthand love sets our sights on continuous nourishment that adjusts to the ebb and flow of life to ensure that we're taking care of ourselves. We're in control of how we love ourselves.

Getting the women I loved to the cabin was underway. The invitations went out to celebrate my fortieth birthday. Twenty women confirmed their attendance. The God idea was in progress. I planned three breakfast, lunch, and dinner menus, eight lesson plans, and five activities. The cabin town is rural, so sourcing vendors for the china, tables, and linens was going to be a challenge, but I was able to identify a company forty-five minutes away that serviced our area. I was attentive to every detail. It was of utmost importance to me that these women have an experience of a lifetime. It was time to pull out my handy-dandy glue gun! I wrapped the gifts I'd bought for the women, created menu cards for all the meals, and made custom napkin rings.

My Authentic Self

Five days before the retreat, I made my Costco run for the groceries and flowers, loaded up my Chevy Suburban, and headed down Interstate 95 south so loaded down with supplies that I had no visibility out my back window. After I hauled in a mountain of bags, boxes, and cases of drinks, I sat down and organized my plan of execution. Every day I would work on a specific area of preparation. Day one, I cleaned the cabin and put fresh linens on the beds. Day two, I rearranged the living room and staged the gifts. Day three, I made the floral arrangements, including personalized ones for the bedrooms. Days four and five, I started prepping the food.

As I mentioned, I wanted the women to feel celebrated, and

nothing says celebration like a cake! On day five, I stayed up until 2:00 a.m. baking individual sweet potato pineapple upside-down cakes with cream cheese frosting. I envisioned a moment when I would present the women with their cakes, each with a sparkler shooting out of the center. (Spoiler: Let me tell you, that moment did not disappoint! The looks on their faces were priceless. What I did not take into account was the sparks from the sparklers dropping on my hand as they were being presented. Those little stings were totally worth it.)

When the day of the retreat arrived, I started getting butterflies in my stomach. The planning and preparation part was easy. Well, maybe not easy—more like easygoing. All the work leading up to the retreat was behind-the-scenes, activities that I was good at and that I enjoyed doing. Truthfully, this was starting to feel like an act of firsthand love for myself. It was three nights and four days of getting the opportunity to show up as my authentic self. That statement—to be your authentic self—is a bit clichéd today. It's been used in so many marketing campaigns that it's lost some of its essence. But that call to action should be taken seriously. There is only one of you in the entire world. And there is only one of me. I believe that's what makes me a superwoman: my power to be authentically me. It's not me giving to everyone and everything, leaving nothing left for myself. I recently went through my 1992 high school yearbook. The quote next to my photo says, "I would like to be remembered for being myself."

I had completely forgotten about sharing that statement. It was a reminder that this core belief was woven into the fabric of my being. All along, I've been in pursuit of making this belief come true.

For most of my adult life, I didn't fully know who I was. Well, the time had arrived for me to become *all* of me. I felt like

I was showing up as myself for the first time. No more tucking parts of my story away. No more shame. The plan was to break bread at the table, reveal my battle with depression, and share the lessons I had learned along the way. It was time for me to shed the bondage of shame, fear, and unworthiness.

I believed that my transparency would be freeing for the other women in my life. My courage would serve as a clarion call to activate the courage within them. I knew I had the responsibility to feed them with love, compassion, empathy, and discernment, because I didn't know all of what they would be bringing to the table. Although only they could step on their path to a better life, they wouldn't be on this journey alone. We would be in it together!

The First Retreat

Every day we laughed, cried, and laughed some more. It was so glorious.

Everyone came in sharing their birthday wishes. I would smile, express my gratitude, invite them to indulge in the spread I had prepared for lunch, and welcome them to take a seat at the table. Many of the women were meeting one another for the first time, but you never would have known it. The warm embraces and the sincere conversations conveyed a story of sisterhood. We gathered around the coffee table accented with chocolate-covered almonds, jelly beans, and a flickering candle dispersing warm notes of vanilla into the atmosphere. The retreat was not curated to be a spa experience. My intention was to make the women feel at home. Home is where the heart is, and I desired for them to know that their hearts were safe with me.

When I broke the news that this wasn't a birthday celebration for me but instead a celebration for them, everyone gasped.

"What?" "A celebration for us?" "Is this for real?" This is when the work started.

The first order of business was to go to their rooms to wash away their makeup and to remove their jewelry, including wedding rings. For our time together, we wouldn't be someone's wife, mom, daughter, or coworker. We were the sole focus. Why remove the makeup? I wanted us to see ourselves as beautiful just the way we were. Additionally, it was symbolic of removing the mask we wear so that others cannot not see what's really going on with us. I had mastered the art of wearing a mask. No one had issues with removing their jewelry, but some struggled with removing their makeup. Some had insecurities with skin blemishes and facial features they were covering up. Others felt naked without their makeup. I left them to grapple with their reasons why. As we journeyed throughout the weekend, I was confident they would become comfortable in their own skin.

The second order of business was to agree that we wouldn't talk about our spouses, children, or work. I can't tell you how many times throughout the weekend that I had to bust up these kinds of conversations. Our identities were locked up in all these other things, and we needed to secure the keys to set ourselves free.

On day one, the women were provided with journals to write a list of everything they needed to release, anything that had been holding them back from flourishing. In the instructions I shared, I told them that this list was for their eyes only. Some of them took the assignment more seriously than others, until they realized that we were taking the lists down to the firepit to burn. Once they knew that no one would ever see the list, they grabbed their pens and started writing as if their lives depended on it. Tears streamed down their faces. Audible sobs and sighs filled the space between the lake water crashing onto the rocks. One by one, we threw our lists into the fire. Some quickly walked away and never looked back. Others stood and watched until there was no evidence other than the ashes.

As we gathered back in the cabin, a distinct somberness settled into the room. The conversations were void of laughter. Letting go is hard, even when we're releasing things that hurt us. We become intimately familiar with them, and they attach themselves to our identities. Much like makeup is symbolic of the mask, the parts of our lives that hold us back are like anchors. They weigh us down, but we also wonder what we'll be without them. *What will people think if they see the real me?*

After the women became comfortable seeing themselves without makeup, it was as if they'd forgotten they'd ever had it on to begin with. I heard one woman say, "I love not having to put all that makeup on every day. I feel so free!" Symbolic of putting on makeup, these lists we wrote in our journals consisted of the heartache and pain that we had been putting on every day. The effort to get all made up in the sorrows of life, just to turn around later in the day to wash it off. And doing it every single day! Exhausting. I knew that once we became comfortable with taking it off, the shame, hurt, and feelings of unworthiness would melt away, and we, too, would feel free.

The Healing Meal

There was no better way to shift the atmosphere than to take a seat at the table to eat some blueberry biscuits, vegetable egg scramble, grits, and candied bacon. With gospel music in the background and laughter in the foreground, our spirits were lifted. On the other side of hard work awaits something better. In our case, it was a better life.

I didn't know what to expect at that first women's retreat. I simply knew that I had to do it. Quite frankly, I never could have imagined what took place at the cabin. The experience exceeded anything I could have thought up on my own. Afterward, I was physically tired, but my soul was fully invigorated. The feeling of showing up as all of me was indescribable, but I knew that moving forward, it was my responsibility to maintain the change that took place in me that long weekend.

For my fortieth birthday, God gave me a women's retreat. I'm proud to share that for my fiftieth birthday, I celebrated the tenth year of the women's retreat now formally known as Vincent Country Women's Retreat. I get to continue loving people with the language God has given me to speak.

Over that decade, nearly all the retreats were held at the cabin. I remodeled the bedrooms so that I could bring more women into this healing space (and improve their sleeping conditions). Some women have attended every year since the very beginning, but I always leave space so that others can be brought into the fold as well.

What has amazed me, year after year, is how many of these women have experienced similar traumas in their lives. They've become very successful and accomplished women who, like me, had perfected wearing masks. They had mastered the art of tucking away their own needs and heartache. But as they got comfortable at my retreats, the masks started coming off. They began working to ensure that the inside lined up with what they were projecting on the outside. It's remarkable how resilient and strong women are, mastering life while coping with the traumas that they've experienced.

I'm honored to be part of their healing process. Especially

because, for some of them, these retreats are the main way they address the hard seasons they've endured throughout their lives. Every year, they're nourished and nurtured by those few amazing days. Then they return home with a fresh perspective. None of them show up to enjoy their time at the cabin and then head back to their lives unchanged. Everyone is going home and applying the lessons and doing the work. They come back stronger and stronger every year, even when they face new traumatic experiences or are triggered by something in their lives. They have the benefit of responding through healed eyes and mended hearts.

I've seen how doing this work year after year makes these amazing women more self-aware and resilient. The amount of time that they need to start opening up about their struggles shortens every time I see them. Initially, we would spend the first few days chipping away at the layers and defenses until the evening before the last day, when they're busting open at the seams. But as the years have passed, it takes less chipping. Many of them can open up on day one. They know they need to process and heal, and they're ready to get on with it. It's amazing to witness. I'm extremely proud of all of them. More importantly, I believe that they're proud of themselves!

The components of the retreat have changed too. Topics, meals, discussion formats, and activities have evolved over the past decade. On the second retreat, I gave my guests the same special gift. In chapter 9, I mentioned the love spoon that Desiré gave me. She did this during a time when Troy knew I was in therapy, but the kids didn't. I'd found my way back into the kitchen, and cooking was instrumental to my healing process. In the middle of it all, my daughter gave me the perfect gift, a wooden heart spoon. She didn't know what was taking place with me, so she had no idea how meaningful and powerful that gift was. As I progressed on my healing journey working with women and coaching, I knew that the love spoon was an ingredient to my success and that I wanted to gift it to others. I would say, "This was my weapon of warfare. I hope it will help you identify yours."

There's so much power in being able to recognize the thing that brings you joy. Something that helps to pull you out of difficult circumstances and that keeps you anchored to who you truly are. That's what the love spoon represented for me. I demonstrate the power of the love spoon at every retreat by using it to prepare all the meals we eat gathered around the table. It's my hope that each woman will seek out her weapon of warfare to find her own joy.

The work I do at these retreats and in my coaching practice is more rewarding and fulfilling than I could have ever imagined. If you would have asked young Tommi what life would look like at fifty years old, she definitely would not have described the life Tommi the woman gets to live now.

And to think, she almost didn't make it. Thank God she did.

Food for the Soul, One Dish at a Time

The kitchen has become my sanctuary. It's the place I go for soul food therapy, my personal tool for healing that keeps me anchored to who I am. My life was forever changed when I took the time to learn to embrace my anointing of cooking, accepting true love, and seasoning my life with prayer. To achieve this level of freedom was not free at all. It cost me a great deal. It's an honor to share my bought sense, the lessons I learned, with the women I love, especially because I'd already paid the price. That is the beauty of building the table. Although I realize that everyone's journey to a better life may look different, none of us has to do it alone. My table is set, there are more than enough seats, and there is certainly plenty of food to nourish your soul. And, of course, your belly!

Gathering around the table is such a special way to honor the incredible women who shaped my life, and I love that every dish I make carries their love and wisdom. Food, love, and prayer are still my guiding principles, helping me to create a life filled with rich connections. I find so much joy in sharing meals with others; it's not just about the food but also about the warmth and care that come with it. The table is my go-to spot for checking in on everyone—offering comfort during the tough times and celebrating the good times. A soul-stirring meal has the power to ease life's challenges and to open up a space for soothing the soul.

As I mentioned earlier, my recipes are like treasured heirlooms passed down through the generations, capturing the heart of my family's cooking tradition. My ancestors didn't jot down recipes; they cooked straight from the heart, teaching me through experience and love. Each dish I prepare is a way to connect my family—both those I know well and those I've never met—through the flavors and memories we share. In every bite, you can taste my family's legacy, reminding us that love knows no bounds and brings us together at the table in spirit and in flavor.

Thank you for joining me at the table, meeting the remarkable women who raised me, and joining us for a nourishing meal. My prayer is that my story was an encouragement to you. I hope it stands as a reminder to keep writing and penning the narrative that makes you proud, healed, and authentically *you*.

Conclusion

The Table Is Set

Now that you have the legacy-inspired recipes for a full table, I hope that you'll take the time to set your own. Developing a consistent practice of nourishing your soul will assist you in living a better life. I became a chef because I love to feed people. I became a life coach because I love to feed people. I've shared these stories and recipes with you now because I love to feed people, even those I may never meet in person. Enjoy the food and life recipes from my table to yours.

Writing this book has been both challenging and healing. There were stories I had forgotten, and the writing process allowed me to see them through my healed eyes. Talk about a new perspective! I hope that reading it has added value to your life and that it's been just the thing you needed to open your eyes to see yourself. You're worthy. Know it. Own it. Live it.

Cooking is the gift that keeps on giving. Make sure, after you finish building your table, that you add a few more chairs to offer this gift to someone else who needs their soul nourished and a big old Nana Edie hug!

I pray that you move forward with intention, building a table filled with dishes that nourish your soul—each one prepared from the distinctive ingredients of your life. May you receive healing in every bite!

About the Author

Tommi A. Vincent is a thought leader and a passionate advocate for women, dedicated to empowering individuals and driving the movement to end domestic violence. As a sought-after public speaker, she brings a wealth of experience to diverse topics, including women's empowerment, flexible goal setting, effective leadership, parenting, marriage, and the art of choosing impact over being right. She also shares strategies for navigating life transitions with minimal disruption. In addition to her public speaking, Vincent coaches women on cultivating emboldening lifestyle habits, helping them unlock their potential and live with greater confidence, purpose, and resilience.

Passionate about sharing hard-won insights, Vincent has delivered keynote speeches for high-profile platforms, including Fortune 100 companies. Her work has been widely recognized in leading media outlets such as the *New York Times*, *Waymaker*

Journal, *Savoy Magazine*, Hallmark *Home & Family*, Andscape, CBS, NBC, FOX, ABC, and WGN.

Numerous community and civic groups have also recognized Vincent with prestigious accolades, including the 2022 Advocate of the Year by Women Against Abuse; 2022 Champion Award by The LOHM; 2022 Women of Impact Award by *IMPACT Magazine*; 2023 Black Girl Magic Award by Urban Word NYC; 2023 Innovative Women in Community Award by Spectrum Circle; 2023 WANDA Food Shero Award; and 2023 Just Call Me Chef Maven Makes Moves Award.

A survivor of domestic violence herself, Vincent brings both personal insight and professional expertise to her work. She serves on the board of the National Domestic Violence Hotline and Survivor Justice Action, guiding public policy and initiatives that provide essential services such as shelter funding, crisis counseling, and safety planning. She is deeply committed to helping survivors transition from merely surviving to thriving, and she works to erase the stigma surrounding domestic violence so that individuals and families can access the resources they need to heal. Vincent's personal mission is to normalize the conversation, not the behavior.

In 2023, Vincent and her husband, Troy, executive vice president for the National Football League, established the Vincent Commission in partnership with Niagara University. The commission includes research and education efforts centered on the perceptions, experiences, knowledge, perpetration, and victimization of gender-based violence among college students.

In addition to her advocacy, Vincent is the host of the *Stay a While* podcast, creating a space where women are encouraged to prioritize their mental health. She emphasizes that "the one unifying factor in every aspect of your life is you—so it's critical to ensure that you're good." Drawing from her experiences with depression, she often incorporates lessons learned from her grandmother Nana Edie, whose love and wisdom centered around cooking and family gatherings. Whether through workshops or coaching sessions, she uses food as a tool for healing, bringing people together around the table to foster authenticity, vulnerability, and meaningful connections.

Vincent is also the cofounder and chief operating officer of Vincent Country, a lifestyle brand that celebrates the strength of the Black family and promotes the values of faith, family, and food. Through this platform, she offers transformative life coaching, including an annual women's retreat, where attendees receive practical tools and emotional nourishment over shared meals. Her mission is clear: to uplift women, foster healing, and empower families to thrive in every aspect of life.

When she's not speaking, coaching, or cooking, Vincent enjoys spending time with her family, making memories with her husband, their children, and loved ones through Vincent Country adventures.